Living Through the Pain

Living Through the Pain

The Lonely Me
A MEMOIR

CATHY A. KURTZ

Living Through The Pain ~ The Lonely Me
A MEMOIR
Cathy A. Kurtz

©2014 Cathy A. Compton Kurtz
All rights reserved.

Hardcover ISBN: 978-1-939288-45-5
Paperback ISBN: 978-1-939288-44-8
eBook ISBN: 978-1-939288-46-2
Library of Congress Control Number: 2013957266

www.CathyAKurtz.com
author@cathyakurtz.com

Published by Healing Hart Publishing,
An Imprint of Wyatt-MacKenzie

Acknowledgement

This book is dedicated to my parents, Dewey and Curtis, who provided me with a Godly foundation; to my wonderful husband Dusk, who supports and encourages me; and to my son, Nick, who has provided purpose to my life; and most importantly to God, who watches over me and is using me in this book to touch and help others. In addition I want to honor my sweet, dear friend Lala, who was a constant friend in my life for twenty-eight years. In 2013 she passed away at the age of ninety-nine. Rest in peace my dear friend and my dear family members.

CONTENTS

Preface ix

CHAPTER 1 My Story 1

CHAPTER 2 My Family 6

CHAPTER 3 Week Before the Fateful Accident 13

CHAPTER 4 The Day Prior to the Accident 20

CHAPTER 5 The Day of the Accident 25

CHAPTER 6 The Next Seven Days 33

CHAPTER 7 Living Alone 41

CHAPTER 8 My Last Summer at Home 53

CHAPTER 9 Away at College 60

CHAPTER 10 The Wedding and Honeymoon 72

CHAPTER 11 Our Married Life 1980–1985 77

CHAPTER 12 The Affair That Ended the Marriage 80

CHAPTER 13 The Hunger 86

CHAPTER 14 The Struggle to Press On 88

CHAPTER 15 Slowly Unraveling 94

CHAPTER 16 The Long Painful Trail 100

CHAPTER 17 The Next Wave Hit 106

CHAPTER 18 Another Door Closes 109

CHAPTER 19 Final Closure 120

CHAPTER 20 A Door Opens and Quickly Closes 125

CHAPTER 21 God's Blessing 130

CHAPTER 22 Trusting God 137

CHAPTER 23 Finding Strength from God 146

CHAPTER 24 My Never-Ending Love for My Father 160

CHAPTER 25 Lessons Learned 166

CHAPTER 26 Moving Forward 169

Photo Collection 173

Preface

"Our greatest glory is not in ever failing, but in rising up every time we fail."

Ralph Waldo Emerson

This book deals with the tragedy and pain I endured. It clearly explains you can't outrun your shame and guilt. I had been raised a strong Christian, yet in my shame, I turned away from God, only barely reaching out to Him from time to time in true desperation. It was only when I was fifty that I finally started seeking God at a deeper level in my life. I realized He had always been there, carrying me most of the time, never abandoning me and, yes, He had long forgiven me of my sins. I had just not learned how to forgive myself.

My life has been a long and difficult journey, but I finally arrived at a place where I can find peace at the end of the road. I am still growing every day, but I now grow together daily with God instead of by myself. I hope you will read my book and join me in my painful journey to find peace in my soul. My wish is that my story may help you put your life into perspective and turn toward God regardless of what journey you are on—you are never alone.

CHAPTER 1

My Story

*"To everything there is a season, a time for
every purpose under heaven."*

Ecclesiastes 3:1

My book begins with a short story I wrote in my senior high school English class almost exactly one year to the date of the fatal accident.

"The Lonely Me"
10/12/77

A lonely figure kneeled quietly in the dark, whispering prayers as tears streamed down her frightened face. That lonely face belonged to me as my disillusionment was stirred about a year ago.

The weekend had started off quite pleasant. My acceptance on the tennis team sent a thrill through my heart early Friday morning. Excited, I hurried home to tell my mom the good news. As usual, everyone was too busy to listen. With the pain building inside, I quietly

Cathy A. Kurtz

walked to my room to pack for our trip. At around five o'clock we drove out of the driveway leaving behind a cuddly white, Alaskan Husky and his companion, a golden-brown miniature German Shepherd.

We drove to the airport and met my brother Ronnie and his wife. My brother had been a pilot for quite some time now, and I was confident of the trip that lay ahead. We were to fly to A&M to celebrate my brother's twenty-first birthday, and there I would remain for the weekend while my family flew on to Dallas for a convention.

That night was a memorable occasion. At dinner the family sat around the table eating with cheery smiles bursting from their faces. However, outside a thunderstorm came echoing through the walls on my brother's trailer. I could almost feel the nerves tightening as fear swept over me. I knew my family was to fly to Dallas in a small twin-engine plane, and the storm was steadily growing worse. After a family council, we were convinced it would be best if they left early the next morning. Dawn woke on a harsh day ahead that would seem to me like an eternity.

Before I awakened, my family had left the trailer and taken off at the airport. Around ten o'clock, my brother woke me to tell me that my parents had not arrived in Dallas. As my body trembled, a sudden presence engulfed me. I knew what had happened, yet I could not admit it! After a telephone call to the Federal Aviation Administration (FAA), my brother and I were informed that the wreckage had been found with people still alive. Panic cringed in our bones as we slowly broke down.

Living Through The Pain

A friend drove us to the site of the accident, but we could only talk to the police, who refused to let us go out to the wreck. After being instructed to go to the hospital, we sobbingly drove off. Little did we know that a four-hour wait lay ahead of us. Finally we were told to go to the funeral home where they were being taken care of. Four thin black bags were lying in an open garage as we drove into the driveway of the funeral home. We knew that they were all dead. For the first time a queasy feeling swept through my body as I was shaking. Sweat poured off my forehead, mixing with the stream of tears running down my face.

Questions, questions, and even more questions! Where was your father born? What was your mother's maiden name? How old was your brother? Your sister-in-law's full name is what? After the death certificates were filled out, a long trip home awaited my brother and me.

That night became a nightmare. The news reports, the telephone calls, the people who dropped by made me want to scream. Sleep would take control of my body every now and then, but nightmares would appear and I suddenly found myself sitting straight up in bed screaming at the top of my lungs. Why? Why them, God? It has to be a lie. Why?

The next week was traumatic. At sixteen I had to face adult problems. Friends deserted me in my time of need, school work was slowly piling up, and the house needed attending to, but sorrow kept me strangely staring into space.

Well, after almost a year now, the pain still exists.

The reality is still there, but probably will never be completely faced. At times I hear my mother call me and I come running only to discover it is my imagination. I cannot say if it will ever get easier, but the pain still exists as if it was yesterday. I guess the hardest thing was to grow up overnight, but when one has no choice, there is not much one can do. Without a mother or father to guide me, a brother to tease me, or a sister-in-law to talk to, it is awfully rough at times. My only living brother lives across town, and I live by myself with a small dog as company. The only happiness in my life now lies with my boyfriend Christopher who has led me through an awful lot of hard times when I thought I would not make it. He has helped to make me strong when I am weak and to strive to live for tomorrow.

I hope that the loneliness in me will leave later in life, but right now, I am still that lonely figure kneeling in the dark, whispering prayers with tears streaming down my frightened face.

That was written by me when I was seventeen years old as a writing assignment for school. It is strange to think this paper, which reflects so much personal pain, won me a national writing award and provided me with numerous English scholarship opportunities to various colleges, none of which I accepted; yet, looking back and re-reading it, I now find it hard to understand why anyone who would read that paper couldn't feel my pain and reach out to help me. Here it is thirty–five years later, and reading it immediately transports me back to that lonely girl as she is always inside me. Only through the grace of God have I been successful in living through that pain as well as the painful experiences soon to follow. My desire in writing this book is to provide courage to others who face serious trauma in their lives so they, too, can "live through the pain."

CHAPTER 2

My Family

*"Do you know why a car's windshield is so large
and the rearview mirror is so small, because our past is
not as important as our future."*

Source Unknown

My parents were loving people. My mom, Curtis, dedicated her life to her kids as well as supporting my father in his career which was demanding. She was a stay at home mom and always made sure we did our homework, remembered our manners, were respectful to others, and attended church weekly. All of my memories of her were of a dedicated person whose family always came before her own needs and desires. She was an excellent role model for me as she fully supported my father and his career; she was also available if I had a problem or needed help with something. I wish I could say more in-depth things about my mom, but at sixteen I didn't have the time I needed in my later teenage years and early adulthood which is when I would have gotten close to her. I missed a lot by losing out on those years and mourned losing her so early in my life, yet her memory has provided me great strength, courage, and determination.

My father, Dewey, was a radio and television figure throughout the Southwest. He developed the very first call-in radio talk show called *Garden Line* for gardeners and farmers on Houston's KTRH radio station. There wasn't anything my dad didn't know about plants or agriculture. He delighted in helping people with their gardening and ranching problems and was the first to try anything new. He always said if he didn't use it, he wouldn't advertise it. I always admired my dad for his integrity and his desire to find a way to feed the world.

Everywhere we went people recognized my dad. In church, people couldn't help themselves from sending notes down the aisle to my dad or grabbing him right after church, leaving us waiting at the car for long periods of time. I was always proud of my dad and his career, but being the child of a celebrity has a price to pay. My parents always told us we had a responsibility since my father was in the public eye. We always had to conduct ourselves as Christians and never do anything that would bring shame or embarrassment to my father. I didn't mind so much as I had a strong conscience, which meant I was always harder on myself than my parents would have been.

My parents provided an excellent foundation of values to guide me in my life. Those values consisted of honesty, love of God and His word, honor your parents, be true to your word, have compassion for others, be productive and work hard, be ethical, and appreciate nature. As I found early on in life, veering from any of these values would take me down a dark path in life, a path which took me years and a lot of tears to escape.

I was the youngest of three children. Ronnie was the oldest (eight years older than I), Kerry (four years older than I) then there was me, the baby girl. My dad was extremely hard on Ronnie as he wanted to mold him into a replica of my dad. It worked, as when Ronnie graduated from Texas A&M, the college my dad went to, he began working with my dad on the radio and TV shows. I have to admit he did seem like a natural. He was tall, good looking and had an outgoing personality. People flocked to him like a magnet. In the radio and TV community, he became quickly known as "Little Dew."

Looking back, Ronnie set the bar high for Kerry and I. In junior high he medaled in swimming and football. By high school he turned his attention to Reserve Officer Training Corp (or as most people know it, the ROTC) which he loved and was the editor of the high school yearbook. He worked throughout high school and bought his first truck. He was dark skinned, deep blue eyes, beautiful smile, jet black curly hair, and muscular in build. The girls loved him. Girls were always asking him out, which I thought was the coolest thing ever. Besides all of this, he was a protective older brother and he cherished his relationship with his baby sister. I always hoped to grow up and marry someone just like him.

Kerry, on the other hand, was the rebel of the family, always charting his own course and doing the unexpected, but he was a genius. Seriously, he scored almost a perfect score on the SAT. He wasn't too sure what he wanted to do with his life except do the opposite of what my dad wanted him to do. In high school he became the editor of the school newspaper. He was like my dad in that he had a lucky green thumb when it came to gardening, yet he wasn't much interested in it. He was tall, thin, light brown hair and pretty green eyes. He would have been what is commonly referred to as the "black sheep" of the family. Ronnie and I were simple in nature, didn't need much to be happy, and just basked in taking life in and enjoying things, whereas Kerry always wanted the biggest, the best, and the most expensive of everything and, of course, had to be the center of attention.

Then there was me, the baby of the family. I was quiet, on the chunky side by the time I reached high school, and just plain. I wanted to be recognized for myself, yet I always felt I was meant to be seen not heard by my parents. I loved gardening and animals, but I didn't want to follow my dad's career. I was smart and did exceptionally well in school. I graduated from high school with a 4.0, but unfortunately my parents weren't there by that time. This was just the beginning of many major life experiences that couldn't be shared with my parents or my family. This was a sad time in my life as I needed my parents' love, support, guidance, and to know they were proud of me.

As a sophomore in high school I announced to my parents I wanted to major in Marine Biology. This would allow me to study and research organisms and marine life. I loved everything connected to the ocean and felt that a career in Marine Biology would offer me the right exposure studying the ocean and its relationship to man. I was also interested in marine conservation where I could play a role in educating the public, students, and other countries in the importance of protecting our marine life, preventing pollution of our waterways, and understanding the role of the ocean in our lives.

My dad was surprisingly enthusiastic, but my mom was anything but supportive. I had mentioned I wanted to learn to scuba dive, but she wouldn't have any part of it, especially after seeing the movie *JAWS*.

My father had wanted us all to learn to become a pilot. He worked at encouraging us to grow and explore different things. When Ronnie was only nineteen, he sent him to Indiana to auctioneer's school during the summer and he returned a full-fledged auctioneer. It was thrilling to listen to those words roll off his tongue. Ronnie then began taking pilot classes. By late 1976, he already had his twin engine license along with being instrument rated and was working on his jet's license. In the fall of 1976, Kerry had just started aviation school, and here I wanted to branch out and be noticed in a different way. I had absolutely no interest in flying a plane when I could explore the depths of the ocean. That is what my heart desired.

My whole life had been focused on school and making good grades. When I got into junior high, I so wanted to get a job, but my parents wouldn't let me. My dad said there were plenty of things for me to do at home: house cleaning, taking care of the yard and when we went to the farm I helped to cut hay, vaccinate the cows and other miscellaneous farm chores. I didn't mind all that much as long as I was outside and close to nature.

The one plan I did have since I was five years old was to attend Texas A&M where my dad had graduated from. My dad never informed me that up until the mid sixties, girls were not allowed to attend A&M as enrollment was only for boys since it was primarily a military school. With women now attending, my path was clearly set for me. I loved Aggie football and I wanted to go to my dad's school. Some of my earliest memories were of lying on the floor listening to the A&M football game on my transistor radio. Ronnie had graduated from A&M and Kerry was now attending college there.

Going to Texas A&M provided me with an opportunity to attend the Texas A&M, Maritime Academy. A&M had a ship that sailed each semester out of Galveston, TX that was for students studying Marine Biology. For one semester students would sail around the world, work on the ship and take classes. I could only imagine how exciting it would be sailing into foreign ports and learning about distant lands. (Even sounds like a romantic teenager looking for excitement!) I could hardly wait for my future to begin as it looked bright. At least that was before October 1976 when everything in my life suddenly changed and I became lost in a world I didn't know or understand.

My father, mother, brother (Ronnie), and his wife were all tragically taken in a horrific plane crash, leaving behind my brother Kerry and myself. Kerry had just turned twenty-one three days earlier and I was sixteen. Kerry was too young to be taking care of a sixteen–year–old, and I needed the type of support and love I wouldn't find from my brother.

In a short course of time, his love turned away from me and he became cruel, evil, and vengeful. I blamed him at the time for his treatment of me. As I aged and matured, I realized he was just too ill-equipped to deal with the tragedies forced on us, and as time went on, he became mentally ill, was hooked on various drugs, and was a severe alcoholic. Until I could release my anger and forgive him, my life was filled with only tragedy, sadness, enormous loneliness, pain and most importantly working to build a mental wall that would protect and isolate me from others and the pain I had suffered and was continuing to suffer.

I had a so-called boyfriend at the time, which I had dated twice, who became a pivotal person in my life. Unfortunately our relationship piled onto my shoulders unbearable guilt and shame which lasted for the most part of thirty plus years until I could put it into the proper perspective and learn to forgive and let go.

CHAPTER 3

The Week Before the Fateful Accident

"If you are lonely, please know you can find comfort. If you are discouraged, please know you can find hope. If you are poor in spirit, please know you can be strengthened. If you feel you are broken, please know you can be mended."

Created for Greater Things, Jeffrey R. Holland

Almost every weekend my family drove to East Texas to manage our two hundred acre farm. We raised cattle, had a few horses, and grew peaches. Being an active teenager, I tried to get out of going on these trips when possible as I was at the age I wanted to be around my friends. The blue skies, green rolling hills, the smell of fresh cut hay, and the endless stars in the night sky are some of my most favorite memories as a child and teenager. On this particular

October weekend, my parents were going to our ranch Friday afternoon and would be back Saturday evening, so they agreed that I could spend the night at my girlfriend's house.

My girlfriend, Casey, and I had planned on going to a local dance where we could see some of our friends and have some fun. Casey was like the sister I never had and, as a result, we did everything together. We both were good kids who never got into trouble and never pushed the boundaries. My mother knew we were going to the dance, but I don't think she was worried too much as she knew I was not the type of kid who would dream of doing something inappropriate.

While at the dance I hooked up with Christopher. I think any smart girl would have known and understood the forbidden rule of not dating your best friend's ex, but not me. I was so insecure about myself, always feeling ugly and having the feeling that I would never have any guy like me, that I found myself falling all over Christopher. Surprisingly, Casey didn't mind, or at least she never acted like she did, and she never told me it was a problem.

The year before, Casey and I had met Christopher. He was a tall blonde, green-eyed cowboy six years older than us. We both fell in love with him; teenage girls fall in love so easily. I was convinced that he liked me as he always hung around Casey and me. I talked to my mom about him and she said a guy will never make a move with two girls together. She advised that I needed to go to the (community) pool sometime without Casey. Well, unfortunately, Casey went one weekend I was at our ranch and wouldn't you know it, that's when Christopher and she hooked up. I was devastated.

I never told her how I felt as I was sincerely happy for her, but this only reaffirmed my feelings of inadequacy. Of course, Christopher would choose Casey over me. She was cute, thin, and had incredibly long, dark, shiny hair and had a bubbly personality. Bottom line, she was a knockout over me. I saw myself as an average, chunky teenage girl, not the kind a guy would look at twice.

After Casey broke up with Christopher, he started to show an interest in me and I jumped on it. On the surface I assumed he was the perfect guy. He always had taken Casey places, was buying her flowers, and was always nice to everyone; and he was so cute in his jeans and boots. I should have asked Casey why she broke up with him, but I never did. I just assumed they were wrong for each other and convinced myself he really wanted to go out with me, but had a chance to ask Casey first. Why I didn't focus on the fact that I was his second choice, I don't know; it was just part of the mind game I kept playing with myself, and it was pretty convenient for me to think that way. What I found out later is that Casey broke off the relationship as Christopher wasn't the perfect gentleman he appeared to be and she was smart enough to end it with him.

By the night of the dance, I had only gone to the movies with Christopher once and corresponded with him while he was at college. I should have seen the signs in his letters as he was always writing about other girls and trying to build himself up to me. One afternoon when I got home from school, my brother Ronnie had come by to visit my mom and saw I had a letter from Christopher. Being the protective older brother, he opened the letter and read it and wasn't too happy. He told me to dump this guy as he wasn't interested in me and certainly wasn't the kind of guy I needed to be going out with. He was full of himself. I remember yelling back at him to mind his own business and scolded him not to read my personal mail.

I was crushed, as Ronnie meant the world to me. I was closer to him than I was my parents, and for him not to like Christopher really hurt. Sadly I knew he was right but my insecurities fought back hard and I convinced myself that Ronnie just didn't know Christopher. I felt he was writing about other girls to impress me and make me jealous.

Now here I was at the dance and Christopher was there. Christopher always liked to act bigger than he was so, of course, he was drinking and spiked my drink. He handed me a Bourbon and Coke. It was so strong it burned my throat as I drank it. I wanted to impress him, so I didn't say anything. I hated it, but I wanted to look cool.

Casey tried to convince me not to drink it, but again with my insecurities, I kept drinking. This was uncharacteristic for me, as I was always the "good girl." I wasn't the kind of kid who participated in things that I knew I shouldn't be doing. I knew the difference between right and wrong. As a result, I always did what I knew to be right, but as the night progressed I got drunk and, in doing so, I started feeling sick. I suppose every teenager has a rebellious demon inside just waiting to escape, and mine certainly took control of me that fateful night.

I wanted to go home and not go to Casey's house. For one, I knew if I started vomiting, her mother would figure out what had happened and would tell my mom, so I asked Christopher to take me home and told Casey to tell her mom I got sick and had Christopher drive me home. Christopher, being the gentleman that he was, said that he would come into the house to check everything out and ensure no one was there before he left. I felt proud that he seemed genuinely concerned about my safety. I was so naïve.

After he had checked all the rooms in the house, he started kissing me. The room started spinning. Everything seemed like it happened in slow motion. Slowly he began to unbutton my clothes, pull my top off and pants down. Next he unfastened my bra and slowly pushed my panties down to my ankles. Now my body seemed helpless, and I was confused and dazed. I felt flushed yet excited that he wanted me.

The room was still spinning when I felt his warm naked body on top of mine. My chest was pounding as I didn't know what to do. He slid his warm, wet penis over my vagina, and that is when I freaked! Reality quickly set in, and I realized I was in way over my head. I tried to push him off me, but he kept trying to penetrate me. His penis was hard and he kept manipulating it with his hand, trying to get it to slide into my vagina. I started screaming for him to stop and, thank God, he finally did.

Immediately I jumped up and put my clothes on. I was more embarrassed than ever and found myself apologizing to him that I was sorry, as I wasn't that type of girl and didn't want him to think I had done something like this before with anyone else. He didn't say much; he just got dressed and left. I immediately ran into the bathroom and vomited. The room was still spinning and I was so ashamed of myself. I had just been molested and almost raped! I embraced the toilet for a while crying, wondering how could I have let this happen.

In time I made it to my bedroom where I laid in my bed and wept all night. My stomach ached; not because of the booze, but because I had done the unthinkable, but I was truly naïve. Now I wondered if I could get pregnant. We hadn't had intercourse, yet I was scared to death. At sixteen, I should have been wiser about sex. Sex was something my mother never talked to me about. I felt God was going to punish me for this horrible sin and whatever happened is what I justifiably deserved. I had failed myself, failed my parents, and failed God.

The next morning I called Casey and told her what had happened. I didn't share my fear of becoming pregnant as I didn't want her to know just how uneducated I was about sex. She had a couple of older sisters so I knew she was wiser than me about sexual things. She did voice her disappointment in me and finally told me that he had made the move on her and, when she rejected him, he got angry. She immediately ended the relationship. I wish I had been as wise as she had been, but I had let it go much farther based on my insecurities, and I felt so much shame and guilt.

When my parents arrived home, I wanted to tell my mom, but I knew if I did, she would never trust me again, and that fear overrode my desire to come clean with her. I did, however, tell her that Christopher had brought me home because I had gotten sick. He had come in, checked out the house, and stayed with me for a while to make sure I was going to be okay, and then he left. It was a good thing I told my mom this story up front as our neighbor called my mom on Monday and told her I had come home on Friday night with a young man who was at the house for about thirty minutes, then left. Since my story seemed plausible, my mom never questioned me.

Even though my parents never knew the truth, the guilt haunted me, and the shamefulness was weighing heavy on my shoulders. I knew it was just a matter of time and I would tell my mom, but I needed to wait to have the courage to tell her as I hated to see what the outcome was going to be. I knew Christopher would be in big trouble for molesting me, but I was more fearful to see the disappointment that would have been in my mom's and dad's eyes. Little did I know how this guilt and shame would play such a vital role in my life for the next several years because I never had that conversation with my mom.

CHAPTER 4

The Day Prior to the Accident

"Most important things accomplished in the world have been accomplished by people who have kept on trying when there seemed to be no hope at all."

Dale Carnegie

Friday, October 15, 1976 seemed like any other typical school day. It was cloudy and cool that morning when I drove to school. Later in the day, I found out I was selected for the high school tennis team. I have never been so proud of myself, yet truly disappointed as Casey wasn't chosen for the team. We both had practiced together days on end to make the team. This moment of achievement for me was bittersweet. I drove home all excited to tell my mom the news, but when I arrived home, she was busy rushing around getting ready for our trip that weekend.

Living Through The Pain

Our plan was to fly to College Station where my brother Kerry attended Texas A&M. The thirteenth of the month had been his twenty-first birthday, so the plan was to stop there and celebrate his birthday, then go on to Dallas for the State Fair. At the Fair, my dad had an agricultural exhibit about the native plants of Israel and showing how the Israelis were using hydroponics.

Initially the plans were that Casey would go with us, but her mom wasn't comfortable with her flying in a small plane. When those plans fell through, Kerry got me a date for the Texas A&M versus Baylor football game on Saturday and asked if I could spend the weekend. I was thrilled as there was nothing I loved more than Aggie football. I was surprised that my mom said yes. This would be the first college football game I had attended at Kyle Field. Fall Saturdays for me were always spent either in front of the TV watching the Aggies play or I would be intensely listening to them on my transistor radio.

Upon arriving home that afternoon, there never was an opportunity to share my accomplishment with my mom, so I went to my room and did what I always did when I was upset; I called Casey. I was packing while talking on the phone to her. When my dad got home, he was angry that he found me on the phone. He didn't understand teenage girls in the least and didn't care to. He yelled for me to get off the phone and help get things ready. As any typical teenager would do, I got mad and clammed up. No way was I going to share my news now.

This hurt me, as this was the first time I had done

something that would set me apart from my brothers and I wanted my parents to know of my accomplishment, but I told myself they would find out soon enough as I wasn't going to share something this important with people who didn't seem to care. Looking back, it all seems pretty petty, but for a teenager, this was a huge event in my life and no one knew.

I was steaming all the way to the airport. When we got there, we loaded our bags into the plane and took off. The weather was beginning to get stirred up by then. It was around 5 PM and the wind had greatly picked up, the dark grey clouds were rolling in, and the temperature was dropping. I had flown with my brother numerous times and always enjoyed flying with him, but this time was different. We were being bounced around like a tennis ball in the air, and I quickly vomited in the back of the plane. It was pretty intense in the plane as no one was talking except my dad and Ronnie, and I couldn't tell what they were saying, but I felt we were in trouble. We all shared a sigh of relief when the tires touched the ground. Ronnie, as always, had come through and we were safely on the ground.

Kerry was there to drive us back to his two bedroom trailer house. I loved his home as I knew when he graduated, the plan was for me to move into the trailer and I couldn't wait. I was ready for my independence.

Kerry had fixed us a nice dinner. I remember a lot of joking and laughing throughout dinner. Outside, though, the storm was stirring. Every crackle of thunder sent a chill through each of us and the thunder seemed to echo loudly off the metal walls of the trailer. It was unspoken, but we all were worried about the trip that faced them going to Dallas. After some deliberation, my dad finally decided the best plan was to wait it out until early morning, then they would leave. He called his contact in Dallas and told them.

Kerry and I were then off for a concert to pick up his date and mine. Once we all got together, the decision was made we wouldn't go to the concert after all. Instead, we would go to the Dixie Chicken, a small, popular local bar/hangout for the college kids. We all had some Lone Stars (another stupid move on my part, but again I was striving to fit in), talked and danced for quite a while, then we went back to Toby's house. Toby was my date.

Kerry and his girlfriend immediately went upstairs and started making love. It was embarrassing to listen to them while we were sitting downstairs. Toby and I didn't have a lot in common, so there wasn't much for us to talk about, so we focused on his fish tank and talked about tomorrow's football game.

I kept watching it get later and later and was concerned that with us going to get in so late and with Kerry being so drunk, my mom would definitely change her mind and make me go with them to Dallas. Toby and I talked until we both fell asleep leaning against one another on the couch when Kerry and his date finally came downstairs. It was around three in the morning. Toby drove us home and we quietly slipped in while everyone was still sleeping.

I couldn't figure out why Kerry decided to start cleaning up the kitchen, banging things around. I told him to be quiet as he was going to wake everyone up. Sure enough, my mom got up. Luckily, she never paid attention to what time it was. She asked if we had a good time, then told us to go to bed. I don't remember where Kerry slept; I assume either on the floor or in a chair as I slept on the couch as both of the bedrooms were full.

CHAPTER 5
The Day of the Accident

"Even in our worst hour, God is with us, always."
Cathy Kurtz

Sometime around six in the morning, according to Kerry, Ronnie picked me up and carried me back to his bed before they left for the airport. I vaguely remember being moved, but was so tired I never woke up.

At around ten that morning Kerry came in and woke me up. He seemed distraught and panicky. He told me the guy whom my parents were to meet in Dallas had called and indicated they were late, they had never showed up. My heart sunk deep into my chest. It was almost an immediate reaction as I could feel my heart pounding hard in my chest. I asked if he had called the airport to see if they got off late or if they had had some problems.

While I was in the bathroom washing my face I heard an awful cry—it was Kerry! I knew it wasn't good. I began shaking and walked slowly down the hall to his bedroom.

— 25 —

He stood there frozen, just staring at the wall. I asked what was wrong and he said the airport told him there had been a crash and it was Ronnie's plane. They had identified the plane numbers. He was told where the accident was and that emergency personnel were responding.

I quickly ran back to the bathroom and threw up. I was crying and shaking, telling myself this couldn't be happening; but maybe everyone is alright after all. Ronnie was a great pilot. I felt like I was in a haze, dreaming a horrible nightmare and couldn't wake up.

Kerry contacted his friend up the street, Bob, who came and picked us up as Kerry was too shaken to drive. We drove about twenty minutes out of town and came upon an emergency vehicle on the side of the road. We pulled over and went up to the man who was standing there. We asked if this was where the plane wreck was and he said yes. We looked out over this ranch and saw nothing. There was just rolling hills, cattle, and a fine mist of rain coming down. It was eerily cold, quiet, and gray. I remember my knees shaking and feeling like I was going to pass out.

He told us the wreck was farther out in the field, and it was so boggy, they needed a special type of vehicle to get out there as anything else would get stuck in the mud. I yelled at him, "Well, why aren't you out there helping them? They must be cold and confused and need help. They need to know we are here and that help is coming!" He said he had to wait for the emergency people to show up.

I started to take off running toward the barbed wire fence, but before I reached the fence, the man quickly tackled me. I fell hard onto the wet ground and was crying uncontrollably. I knew he felt bad and that he was doing his job, but this was my family! He held me and wouldn't let me go. I was crying, screaming, and yelling for my mom, but he held tight. He told Kerry to take me to the hospital and wait for my parents to be brought there.

Bob and Kerry carried me to the car. We all sat in the front seat as I wept hysterically. I kept asking why no one was going out there to help them. I know Mama would be worried about us and she needed our help. Kerry said the best we could do was go to the hospital and wait. They would bring them there as quickly as they could. He agreed that with us being at the site we would be in the way and slow the emergency workers down. I asked if he really thought they were alive and he said yes since we were told to go to the hospital. I kept changing the dial on the radio frantically, trying to see if there were any news reports that could tell us anything more than what we had been told. There was nothing; only the eerie announcements that Dewey Compton's private plane had crashed and no word yet on any survivors.

When we arrived at the emergency room, we went to the nurses' station and told them who we were. They asked us to take a seat. From what I remember, the seating was just inside the door of the emergency room, and people kept coming in banged up pretty bad. The constant smell of the hospital made me sick as well. I had never been in an emergency room before, so the whole experience was traumatizing.

Every time I heard an ambulance pull in, I jumped up and ran outside, but it was never my family, always someone else's. At one point, I remember a man coming in and sitting beside us. He was distraught. I asked what was wrong and he said his son was in a car wreck and he had no idea how he was. I told him I would pray for his son. Hours went by and finally the man was informed his son would be fine. He had some minor cuts and bruises and two broken arms, but all in all he was quite lucky. I was happy for the man and hoped our outcome would be the same, yet we continued to wait. By now it seemed we had been there all day with no news. I was exhausted, numb; my eyes were swollen and I felt I was going crazy. I wasn't sure I could take much more.

Periodically I would get up and ask the nurses, actually demand, that the nurses give us an update. It was always the same; they hadn't heard anything, but as soon as they knew something, they would let us know. I didn't trust them; actually I didn't trust anyone as I felt they were all lying to us. I felt they knew something, but refused to tell us.

Finally something came through on their hospital radio about a plane crash and the nurse quickly turned the volume down. A few minutes later two Catholic nuns came out to meet with us. When I first saw them, I knew this meant they were dead. By the time they knelt in front of me I was in total hysteria. They gently tried to calm me down by telling me my family was fine. They held my hands and prayed with me. They told my brother the name of a local funeral home and said they were taken there as it was the closest place to take them for help. I asked help? What type of help? They indicated medical help. They assured me they were all fine.

At this point I was so confused. I wasn't Catholic, yet I did respect the Catholic faith and felt that nuns most certainly couldn't or wouldn't lie, yet what type of medical services could a funeral home offer my family? It had been four long grueling hours at the hospital and I was exhausted, both emotionally and physically. Bob and Kerry helped me up and supported me as we walked slowly to the car. I halfway began to smile and said well, maybe it will all be okay, do you think so? Both Bob and Kerry were quiet. I knew they were exhausted as well, so I decided to be quiet, which was probably what everyone wanted, just some quiet for a few moments.

After a brief drive, we slowly turned into the long gravel driveway of the funeral home. Directly in front of us was a large garage and the big doors were open. Much to my astonishment, there laid on support tables were four white pine boxes (In my high school class story, I don't know why I referred to them as black bags except referring to boxes may have been too difficult for me to say at the time). Immediately I panicked. I yelled, "They lied to us! How can nuns lie? This is so wrong. That can't be them. Oh God no, please no!" I noticed it was still raining, and I thought Heaven must be crying for my family.

Kerry never said a word; he just helped me out of the car and we slowly walked to the back door of the funeral home and walked in. My heart was pounding so hard in my chest that I could hear every heartbeat. I remember a large room to the left of us with large windows which had black curtains drawn, preventing us from looking inside.

Kerry said someone would have to identify the bodies,

so if that was the case, he would do it and I would need to stay out in the hallway with Bob. I told him no, I wanted to go in and started to reach for the door handle, but he knocked my hand away. At that moment a tall, middle-aged man came out and greeted us. He asked us to join him in the parlor. Parlor? Who says parlor? It was all too creepy.

The house was an older home and the furnishings were more on the antique side of things. It actually smelled a little musty in there, the lights were dimly lit and I felt uncomfortable. The gentleman naturally thought someone had informed us that our family members were dead but he didn't know what we had been told at the hospital. He immediately began running down a list of questions from his clipboard and I freaked. He was asking, "What is your father's middle name, your mother's maiden name, their birth dates, places of birth, etc.?"

Kerry was quiet and didn't say a word. I was shocked and angry. I told him that I refused to answer any questions as our family was not dead; there had been a horrible mistake. I knew they were still alive out there and trying to get a hold of us. The man responded I couldn't see them as it would be detrimental for me to see them the way they were. I demanded again that I wouldn't cooperate as it wasn't them. He indicated he had an idea and excused himself.

The three of us sat silently, no one moving. My body was trembling with fear and I felt cold, so very cold. The man finally returned, placing in my hand my father's bloody and muddy Texas A&M college class ring with his name

Living Through The Pain

engraved on the inside. It was definitely my dad's ring and it was covered with the smell of death. Tears welled up in my eyes, and I quickly asked for the bathroom. He walked me to the bathroom in a rapid manner as I barely got there in time and started throwing up into the sink. I must have stayed in the bathroom about fifteen minutes throwing up, crying, and washing my face with cold water. I looked in the mirror and told myself this couldn't be happening. This must be a horrible nightmare and I just haven't woken up yet.

Finally I returned to the parlor and sat down. I was ready to surrender to the inevitable, so I began to answer his questions for the purpose of filling out the death certificates. The questions went on for about an hour. Kerry must have been in shock as he never said a word. I answered all the questions. When the man was through, he said he would coordinate to get the bodies to Houston, but he would need a contact. Kerry told him he or someone else would get back to him.

We left in total silence, moving slowly to the car. My legs shook and my whole body trembled. All the way back to the trailer no one said a word. I couldn't even cry as I was so exhausted. I kept looking at my dad's ring, the only thing I had left of him. At that point I had run out of tears. It all just didn't seem real. How could it be? This just couldn't have happened. How did it happen and why? They were such good Christian people and were always helping people. Why?

When we got to the trailer, I remember telling Kerry we needed to call our grandparents and tell them along with our aunts and uncles so they didn't see it on the news. I called part of the family and he called the others. This was hard to do and again didn't seem quite real to me. I don't even remember what I said; I just remember making the calls.

When I was through, I went to lie on the couch. Kerry told me to lay down on one of the beds but I didn't want to be in a room by myself. I already was feeling quite lonely inside. I nodded off and on until about ten o'clock when Kerry turned the evening news on. The headline story was about the plane crash. They blamed my brother Ronnie, indicating he had apparently lost control of the plane. That was like stabbing my heart. Ronnie did no such thing, I cried out! The news showed pictures of the crash site, and all that could be seen was the tail of the plane sticking out of the ground. The reporter said the plane had been flown full-throttle into the ground. Then the reporter held up my dad's driver's license. How could they let a reporter out there and not us, and how could someone get anything that belonged to my dad? I felt so betrayed by everyone and so angry. I started crying hysterically again, and finally Kerry made me take a Valium. It wasn't long after that that I simply drifted off to sleep on the couch. My nightmare had only just begun to unfold.

CHAPTER 6

The Next Seven Days

*"How long must I wrestle with my thoughts and every
day have sorrow in my heart?"*

Psalm 13:2

Most everything about the next seven days seems like a complete blur to me. There are a lot of missing pieces for me as I simply can't remember. My first recollection is of Kerry leaving College Station early on Sunday morning. He wanted to get to our home in Houston, before I got there and let our relatives in and get things settled down before I arrived. Toby offered to drive me back to Houston and we got there a little before noon. I remember turning down the street and seeing a lot of cars and people in our front yard. I quickly realized I wasn't ready for what laid ahead of me. I didn't want to see people right now; it was going to be hard enough to walk into our home without our parents being there.

When I got into the house, there were so many people, and they kept hugging me and crying and saying they were sorry. I also remember quite a few people telling me in time it would get better. I wondered what they knew about me and how I would process all of this. I thought they were simply foolish people and how I wished they would all go home. Get over this; how the hell does a person ever get over this?

When I got to my bedroom, there were a lot of kids from my high school there. Many weren't even close friends. It was nice to see them, but I was shocked they were in my bedroom. That was my private space, and I didn't want people invading my privacy. I was so embarrassed and also didn't want my friends to see me this way. It was hard on them as well, as no one said anything, at least not that I remember. I just remember them all staring at me. I felt like a freak.

At some point Christopher arrived and I felt I could at least escape with him to the back yard and have some quiet time. We were sitting in the swing talking. He was holding my hand, and my aunt walked outside and saw us. She came up and told us now was not the time to be affectionate with one another. We needed to stop holding hands immediately! It was at the particular instance that the shock wore off and I remembered the couple of weeks prior, the sexual escapade in my family room with Christopher! Oh no, this is why I lost my family. God is punishing me! It all came back now.

I suddenly felt sick and had to go inside and throw up. My heart was pounding. What would I do? How could I ever tell anyone? The shame and guilt settled over me and engulfed my soul. I should have been in that plane, and I should have died, not them. How could I ever leave the bathroom? When I finally stepped out I told my Aunt I wanted to go to bed and asked that she have my friends leave. Once they were gone, I went to my bedroom, lay in my bed and cried myself to sleep.

The next memory I have is of Ronnie's best friend, Daniel, and his wife driving Kerry and me to the funeral home for a private viewing. It was cold and raining, and I didn't want to go inside. I was so scared. My entire body was shaking. When we got inside, the room they were in was large. I remember how eerily quiet it was. It seemed almost like a huge auditorium. I remember the walls all being lined with flowers, and up front on the stage were four beautiful caskets draped with yellow roses. It all seemed so peaceful. I quickly broke down.

It was hard seeing just the caskets and not being able to see them. I felt so isolated from them. With the caskets being up on this stage, I couldn't even touch the caskets. I felt so sick and so alone and was engulfed with grief and guilt. I remember sitting in the pew and praying to God how sorry I was. Nothing would ever be the same. I don't remember how long we were there; I just remember the feeling of shame and guilt and total sickness running throughout my body.

I asked Daniel if they were really in the caskets and, if so, how do we know that? Can I look and see? He said no there were just black bags in the caskets and the bodies were mangled pretty badly. I asked how badly, and Kerry said they hired someone to determine what pieces went in each bag. I now realize he said this to try and give me some peace of mind but instead I was horrified that they were in pieces. I could only see them as whole bodies in my mind. That was more than enough information for me as I ran out of the room. I went once again to the bathroom and threw up.

My next memory is getting ready for the funeral. The first time a teenager gets to ride in a limousine should most certainly not be for their parents' funeral, but it was for me. The limo was a dark navy blue. Kerry and I didn't want anything to do with black. I suppose it seemed too morbid. Kerry thought it would be helpful if I invited some of my friends to come with us in the limo. I remember Casey and Christopher being there, and it seems like someone else was there, too, but I can't remember seeing anyone's face so I don't know for sure if there was anyone else.

Looking back, what a horrible burden I put on Casey and Christopher. Neither ever complained, and both spent the entire day with me. It was a long day as, after my parent's funeral and burial in Houston, my brother and sister-in-law were to have a funeral and burial service in Beaumont, TX about one and a half hours away. This is where her family was from and we wanted Ronnie buried next to his wife.

At the funeral, we went in through the side door of the church. It was the largest Church of Christ in Houston. This church was chosen to handle the large crowd. Even with that, some people had to stand outside the church as they couldn't get in. Luckily they could hear the services from speakers set up outside the church.

There were news crews everywhere as my father was quite famous in the Southwest and everyone wanted a piece of the story. All I remember was hundreds, perhaps thousands, of people, flowers, and four caskets, four hearses. I thought how these people would feel if they knew my family was dead because of me. I remember sitting in the front pew with my aunt on one side and Christopher on the other. My knees were shaking and I felt sick. It all seems like a blur as nothing is clear about that day. Thinking back, I don't know why Kerry wasn't next to me. It seems like he would have wanted to comfort me or we could try and comfort each other.

The pastor gave the eulogy. The only part I remember is him talking about my mom and dad bringing him an olive wood covered Bible from Israel. He said that was just like Dewey and Curtis, always thinking of others. How true, I thought and how sad their own daughter's sin resulted in their death! I had asked that we sing my mother's favorite song, "How Great Thou Art," and that is when I became hysterical. I missed them so much already and wanted their forgiveness. I didn't mean for any of this to happen.

At the end of the service I was taken to a lounge area while we waited for the caskets to be placed into the hearses. My dad's parents came up to Kerry and me. They wanted to let us know they would be leaving after the burial and wouldn't be going to Ronnie's and my sister-in-law's service as they needed to head back to East Texas to feed the cows. I was stunned. I wasn't particularly close to this set of grandparents, but I never would have thought they would have flaked on Ronnie's funeral. I asked if they were kidding. This was their oldest grandson and they had to feed the cows? My grandmother said yes, they wouldn't be going as it was a long drive back. I dearly loved my mom's parents, but they were way too old to drive down from East Texas. I felt sorry for them having to deal with this by themselves.

As if this wasn't enough of a shock for the day, my grandmother told my brother and me that she and my grandpa knew I would need someone to live with as Kerry would be going back to college. They kindly offered to take care of me if I signed over my part of the estate to cover my expenses. Can you just imagine? My parents hadn't even been buried yet, and this is what my own grandmother thought of me—money! I quickly shouted back, "Don't worry about me, I'll be just fine. I'm not moving to East Texas!" Then I walked off. I was so hurt. This was too much for me to even begin to process. Wow! How cold hearted my own flesh and blood could be at a time like this. Christopher grabbed my arm and escorted me out to the waiting limo as it was time to bury my parents.

When we got to the cemetery, we stepped out of the limo and walked over to the area where my parents were to be buried. The day was cold and overcast, and the wind was blowing. Besides this, I have absolutely no recollection of the burial; I suppose it was too painful to remember, so my brain has blocked the details of the day.

While walking back to the limo, a TV reporter placed his microphone in my face and asked how I was doing. I know my parents would have been horrified by my behavior, but I shoved the microphone out of my face and yelled at the guy, "Get the hell out of here. This is private and I don't plan on sharing anything with you!" Christopher quickly got me into the limo, and Kerry spoke with the reporter. I suppose he was on enough sedatives that he exhibited no emotions and was able to meet with all the reporters until they had the stories they wanted.

I have no recollection of the drive to Beaumont, the funeral service, or the burial for my brother or sister-in-law. I am not surprised as I totally worshipped Ronnie and this would have been too much for me to bear. I suppose my coping mechanism was for my brain to just shut the pain out.

Later that week, Kerry went to pick up the remaining belongings found at the crash site which were being released from the Federal Aviation Administration (FAA). He returned home with Ronnie's college ring, my dad's and Ronnie's wedding bands, my mother's wedding band which was crushed, indicating her finger had been severed, my sister-in-law's necklace that her father had given to her, a pair of bloody tennis shoes that were my mom's, several coins that were bloody and covered in mud and had a smell I will never forget and a pair of my mom's jeans that were torn and bloody. We didn't get any luggage or anything else back. The smell is what I remember most; the smell of death. It was so strong. I will never, ever forget it.

I don't know how many days went by, but the next memory I have is sitting in my parents' living room with Daniel and his wife, my aunt, and Kerry. I knew whatever they wanted to talk to me about couldn't be good. I wondered if they had discovered my secret about Christopher. Would I go to jail? Would they disown me? What was going to happen?

Daniel started explaining that Kerry had to go back to college and I would need a place to stay. I smiled and said, "Well, of course, I will stay here." Daniel explained the courts won't let me live by myself as I am only sixteen. He indicated he knew it wouldn't be perfect, but his mom and dad had offered to take me in. I started crying as I didn't even know them.

I wondered about my friends, my school, and my dogs. Daniel assured me it would be alright. I said no, I wanted to stay here. Everyone agreed I had to live with someone so I thought about one of my girlfriends and asked if I could live with her. Of course no one knew what they would say, so I think they agreed to pacify me and said that would be great if her parents said okay.

Naomi was my friend's name and she was an only child. She was my other close friend whom I met in junior high and I so hoped her parents would take me in. Casey came from a large family, so I knew it would be out of the question for her parents to take me in. I didn't want to change schools. I was so scared; what if they didn't want me?

Kerry called and talked to them and they agreed. I was elated! On Sunday I packed my bags and moved to Naomi's house. Kerry would be home every weekend so I could go back home on the weekends and every day after school I would go home and take care of the dogs. This would become my new life for the next couple of months.

CHAPTER 7

Living Alone

*"Character cannot be developed in ease and quiet.
Only through experience of trial & suffering can the soul
be strengthened, ambition inspired,
and success achieved."*

Helen Keller

Naomi's family was kind and patient with me. Even with their kindness, though, I still felt like I was walking on egg shells. I didn't want to disrupt their family life at all. I was ashamed I had to live with them and they had to change things because I was there. I felt I was infringing on Naomi's time with her parents, and watching their interactions together made me miss my parents even more. I tried not to be in anyone's way. They did everything they could to make me welcome and part of their family, but I simply couldn't cope.

Three weeks after moving in with Naomi, it was my seventeenth birthday. My birthday was such a letdown. It wasn't anyone's fault. Christopher had a nice surprise party for me at his parents' house, but nothing could replace the family that I so desperately missed. All I really wanted was to wake up from this nightmare and my life could continue the way it was supposed to be, but that didn't happen. Kerry was already tired of my crying all the time. He should have understood how I was feeling and realized that I desperately needed counseling. Unfortunately, I think he just felt ill-equipped to deal with his pain and my pain as well.

The next big event was Thanksgiving. What did I have to be thankful for? I wondered. We stayed home that day and kept to ourselves. I remembered wondering how I would go on as the pain was so deep and so severe, I couldn't see myself surviving very long without my family. Finally it was Christmas break. I was miserable living away from home. I begged my brother to let me move back home alone and he finally agreed. He felt I was old enough to handle living by myself, but he would monitor me week by week and, if something changed, I would have to move back in with Naomi's family. I was determined to make this work as I didn't want to ruin anyone else's life. Being alone, I told myself, is what I deserved, especially since I had become so introverted that I hardly spoke to anyone.

Christmas was a painful holiday. We tried to make the best of it, but it just wasn't a pleasant time for either of us. I received more Christmas presents than I had ever gotten before. Kerry tried to make Christmas special, but I could tell he was just trying to buy my happiness for a short while. Considering things hadn't been the best between us, I appreciated his efforts.

Living Through The Pain

School was tough on me as I felt like I had the plague. Everyone stayed away from me, and when friends were around it seemed awkward. No one quite knew what to say, and everyone was afraid of saying the wrong thing so they simply said nothing. I had quit the tennis team as I just didn't have the drive nor desire any longer. I did manage to keep my grades up, but I was miserable and all alone. I didn't have anyone I could share my guilt and shame with.

After school, I went straight home and took care of the dogs, did the clothes, and mowed the yard. I had no time to just be a teenager. I slept with all the lights on in the house as I was scared to be alone at night. The house was engulfed with silence and, for a teenager, it was frightening. I always worried my parents' spirit might return and haunt me for what I had done with Christopher.

For a couple of weeks straight, someone kept getting into our back yard, and each night they would smash one of the plants that had come from the funeral. I didn't know who could be so cruel or why they would do such a thing. This always made me feel like someone was watching me. I never opened the blinds or the curtains and kept the doors locked except when I let the dogs outside. I didn't make a big deal about it, as I didn't want Kerry to make me move, so I just learned to live in fear and remained silent. We had burglar bars on the windows; I had the dogs inside with me along with my mom's 38 Special so I felt I could handle anyone who tried to break in. Nothing about my life seemed normal.

In addition, I never quite understood why no one ever called or visited me or even invited me over for dinner; no family, no neighbors, no one from our church, not my friends' parents, no one. Here my dad was a celebrity whom people adored, yet no one cared about his baby girl. I felt all alone in the world. What was wrong with me? I wondered if they thought death was something they could catch. It was a horrible existence, one that no teenager should have to bear. I simply didn't exist to anyone except myself, and then there was Christopher.

There were times when Christopher and one of his friends would drive over from college at one or two o'clock in the morning. They were drunk. The doorbell would ring and I would panic. Christopher would yell, and I knew it was him and would let him in. He wanted some late night sex. Even though I still refused intercourse, there was the oral sex ritual or manual sex, as I called it. I had no choice as he was persistent. I hated it but I felt trapped. I really didn't know what to do, as Christopher was about the only person in my life and if I lost him, I had no one.

No seventeen-year-old girl should have had to go through what I did much less do so alone. Christopher would get the servicing he wanted, he would kiss me goodbye and leave with his friend. I would stay up, cry all night, and go to school the next morning. To me, living was hell and I had no way to escape. I wondered how my life could have gotten so bad because of one sin. God, can you please forgive me?

I suppose this was the time my creative writing skills finally kicked in. I excelled in English and enjoyed analyzing different novels we had to read. I found I could write passionately about things and was able to easily interpret the characters and what they felt. I now believe this was my way of getting in touch with my own feelings. There was one assignment I had to write based on *Hamlet*. My teacher called me up after class and told me she was giving me an "F" on the paper as it was too good for me to have written by myself. She knew Kerry and felt he had helped me with my paper. I assured her he didn't as he never helped me with anything. I gave her his number and urged her to call him. I don't know if she did or not, but I finally got the paper back with an A on it. I couldn't seem to get a break anywhere.

The following weekend Kerry came home and was fit to be tied. I had no idea what was wrong, but he ordered me to take all the family pictures down and box them up. I was no longer allowed to mention Ronnie's name in the house ever again. I couldn't understand what set him off. He finally told me that he was notified that Ronnie had an insurance policy because he was a pilot. He left a $10,000 insurance policy in my name alone. I started crying as I couldn't believe Ronnie had thought so much about me. Well, Kerry wasn't pleased as he felt this was a slap in his face. After all, he was taking care of me. I told him he could have the money; just knowing Ronnie loved me was all I needed. It didn't matter, as my fate was now sealed with Kerry as he couldn't forgive me for this. This was the beginning of the end of my relationship with him as it quickly deteriorated after this day.

Now Kerry resented having to come home every weekend for his baby sister. He began drinking heavily and taking more and more pills and smoking pot. He became demanding of me. Before he would leave on Saturday mornings (he had taken over my dad's Saturday radio show), he would give me specific instructions on what he wanted taken care of before he came back home that night. His list would consist of things like: move the couch from the garage and place it in the family room (we had Ronnie's furniture in our garage); move the file cabinet into another room; move the bed and dresser here, etc. These were all hard jobs to do by myself, but I did what he asked of me as I was scared not to. I learned to push with my legs (luckily they were strong) and pull. Eventually I found I could move almost anything if I had enough time and patience. As a result of all the pushing and shoving with my knees, I now endure chronic pain from arthritis and loss of cartilage in both of my knees.

I had no choice, as one of Kerry's favorite threats was he would send me to an orphanage and he said he had the legal authority to do so because he was my legal guardian. I lived in constant fear. I didn't complain, though, as I felt this was my punishment—to live in hell.
In addition I had learned I couldn't cry around Kerry. I thought it was normal to cry from time to time, especially around holidays or certain days, but Kerry strictly forbid me from crying. He had gotten good at calling his doctor friend to come over and shoot me up with what he said was Valium if I cried too much.

One time, I was sad and missing my family and I had a mini-break down. I tried not to cry, but the more I tried to suppress it, the louder I became. I started shaking uncontrollably and having problems breathing. Kerry called his "doctor" friend, who gave me some shot while Kerry lay across me to keep me still. Christopher had never seen this before, so he decided on his own to stay. He overheard Kerry telling the doctor that he had had enough of my breakdowns and thought maybe he should send me away to an orphanage or hospital or something as this was too much for him to handle anymore.

When I woke up the next morning, Christopher was lying in bed next to me in just his underwear. I felt defenseless. How could I possibly stop this nightmare? I hated the idea that Christopher was now in my bed in his underwear and I knew this would make Kerry even madder at me. I asked him to leave and, sure enough, he and I both were in trouble except it wasn't with Kerry; it with his dad since he didn't come home all night. I felt his dad thought I was a slut, but I had nothing to do with this. Everything just kept happening around me, and I didn't know what to do or who to talk to.

Christopher going home late or not going home at all started to become a pattern on the weekends. His dad would talk to both of us and scold us and said he had to be the parent and since I was a minor all he could do was put a curfew on Christopher and naturally Christopher would always miss his curfew. I would beg and plead for him to leave. Sometimes he would leave in enough time to get home, but he wouldn't go home. I don't know where he went, but once again I found out we both were in trouble. I think Christopher hoped his dad would kick him out, thus opening the door for him to move in with me, and this terrified me even more.

Then there was Kerry's behavior. I tried to talk to my aunts about Kerry, but they didn't want to get involved in a family squabble. I talked to Christopher's parents about Kerry, but I thought they felt I was crazy as my stories always seemed so bizarre and, besides, at this point I think they thought I was corrupting their son. I couldn't talk to Christopher about my relationship with him as I felt he would just laugh at me. At this point, I wasn't very close to Naomi or Casey or anyone anymore, so I had no one to turn to, and I certainly couldn't turn to God, who was displeased with me.

My relationship with Kerry kept diminishing. One evening I ran out of time to fix dinner and used Hamburger Helper to make beef stroganoff. I knew Kerry felt a meal like this was beneath him, so I felt I could disguise it by adding mushrooms and red wine to it. I tasted it and thought it tasted good.

He got home and was tired and ready to eat. My mistake was throwing the box into the garbage under the sink versus throwing it away in the outside garbage can. He opened the cabinet to throw something away and found the box. He totally flipped out and started yelling at me. "You are nothing more than a fucking bitch! You are totally worthless at everything!" He poured the meal down the garbage disposal and stormed out, leaving me with nothing to eat for dinner.

By the time Christopher got there I was on the kitchen floor crying my eyes out. Christopher's answer, as always, was sex. Again, I felt trapped and totally disgusted with my life. It seemed that all I did was cry or throw up, and I was always clamming up when Christopher or Kerry was around but they were my only contact with the world as I never interacted with anyone else.

One day I returned to school and my English teacher once again called me up after class was over. She had a stern look on her face and told me how disappointed she was in me. She indicated my parents would be appalled at my behavior. I knew she didn't know about Christopher, so I asked what she was talking about. She showed me an article from that morning's newspaper, the *Houston Chronicle*. The article indicated that I had sued my father's company for hiring Ronnie to fly the plane in an incompetent, reckless manner, resulting in the untimely deaths of my parents. The lawsuit was for $400,000. I started crying. I told her I didn't know anything about this, but she didn't believe me. She went on to say that my parents were the nicest people, and she had taught Ronnie and Kerry and how ashamed she was that I would do such a thing for money. I ran out of her class. Luckily it was my last class for the day.

When I spoke to Kerry about it, he said he was doing me a favor. He was my guardian and he was looking out for my best interest as well as his. Our dad's company had insurance, so this was a way to collect the insurance money that was rightfully ours. I yelled back at him, "Sure by blaming Ronnie! What is wrong with you?" He said we aren't technically blaming Ronnie, but rather blaming our dad for his poor judgment in having Ronnie fly the plane. Just think of it, he said, "You being on the stand and crying and all. The jury will fold and give us the money. This will be the easiest money we will ever get in our life." I told him if he went forward with the lawsuit and put me on the stand I would testify against him. I would indicate that I saw this as "blood money" and I would have no part in it.

I remembered that shortly after the accident, Kerry came to me and told me he had placed Ronnie's Flight Log Book in an envelope and had put it under the insulation in the attic. If anyone ever asked about it, I was supposed to say I didn't know anything about it. I don't know how Kerry got it. Maybe he retrieved it with the belongings from the plane crash or maybe Ronnie didn't have it in the plane. All I knew was this seemed odd, but I didn't question it at the time.

Before my parents' house was sold, I went up into the attic and retrieved it. I now think Kerry had planned the lawsuit for quite some time and, without the log book, there would be no way to prove how much airtime/experience Ronnie had. Eventually he dropped the lawsuit, but this left an even bigger rift between us. Now I felt no one at school or in the neighborhood most definitely would ever talk to me again. My life was only getting worse, and I felt I was spiraling out of control.

I needed counseling, but during those days there were no counselors, just psychiatrists, or at least that is all I knew. To go to a psychiatrist would certainly mean I was crazy and would give Kerry the ammunition he needed to just commit me, so I kept all my feelings to myself and focused on school.

Being in so much pain all the time, I came up with the idea that my life would be better if I started college early. I checked with my high school counselor and found out that if I took Economics over the summer, I could graduate the following November and start Texas A&M in January. This would be my new focus. I had no friends anymore, and I hated my life in Houston, so going away to college would be the perfect answer to my problems. Now all I had to do was hang in there until January.

Little did I know, there were still many more trials ahead for me to endure. Christopher and I had made an agreement that we wouldn't have intercourse until my prom night. That was as far as I felt I could stall him. Unfortunately, now that I was graduating early, he pressured me to go to his sister's prom that May since certainly I wouldn't want to come back to my class's prom after I had already started college. I was nervous all night. For one, no one accepted the fact that I was crashing their prom, so in other words I wasn't welcome there; then, as the time ticked away, I knew so were my excuses. I had to give up my virginity and I hated it, but at the same time I couldn't afford to lose Christopher as he was the only person in my life.

That night we came back to my parents' house. Christopher always seemed to have control issues and that night was no exception. He wanted to make love in my parents' bed! This was the worst thing ever. I hated it, but there was no changing his mind. So that is where I lost my virginity, in my parents' bed! At least I insisted he use a condom. It was horrible for me. I simply laid there and let him do his stuff. I could look over and see my parents' picture on their dresser, and it felt like their disapproving eyes were watching me in horror.

He was quite satisfied that I was a virgin.

Later I learned he had been with many girls, one as young as fourteen! I felt humiliated and ashamed, guilty once again in front of God and I hated it. It was many years after this evening that sex ever seemed like "making love." I hated it every time he touched me as I felt it was more of a violation against my body and soul than a perfect union of two people coming together in mutual bliss, but as always I survived that night and moved on, knowing eventually I wouldn't be able to deal with my pain any further. I knew one day emotionally my brain and heart would shatter, but for now I was biding time, just trying to survive.

CHAPTER 8

My Last Summer at Home

*"Tragedy blows through your life like a tornado,
uprooting everything, creating chaos.
You wait for the dust to settle and then you choose.
You can live in the wreckage and pretend it's still the
mansion you remember, or you can crawl from the
rubble and slowly rebuild. Because after disaster strikes,
the important thing is that you move on. But if you're
like me, you just keep chasing the storm."*

Veronica Mars

While I was going to summer school, Christopher had a summer college class at night that he was taking, American History. He had a term paper which required research on the assassination of John F. Kennedy. Christopher didn't like writing, so he asked me to do the research and write the paper for him. Of course I said yes. Writing always took me to a different place, a safe place where I could escape my world, so I didn't mind helping.

One Saturday I was in my parents' office with Christopher working on the paper and he suddenly decided it was time for some oral sex. He got up and closed the door. Kerry was in the house, so I was petrified, but he insisted, pulling down his jeans. Wouldn't you know my luck, just as I got started, Kerry walked in on us! I was scared of what Kerry would do, but he simply shut the door and walked away. I wanted to stop, but Christopher insisted that I finish what I started. Once Christopher was satisfied, I tip toed down the hallway to see Kerry. I wanted to apologize, knowing I was going to get yelled at and I was scared he would now send me away.

With a knot in my stomach and my heart pounding loudly, I could see the light on in my parents' bedroom so I slowly walked up and saw him sitting in the middle of their bed with my mom's 38 Special pointed to his temple. I started crying and asked him to put the gun down. He just stared right through me.

I told him I knew what I had done was wrong and I was sorry. What could I do to make it right? He stated, "Nothing. There is nothing you can do but stand there and watch me. I hate you. I hate you so much that I want you to see me blow my fucking brains out. I know you will go crazy because of this and then you will be paid back for everything you have done as you have ruined my life! I hate you and I hate taking care of you!" I asked him to shoot me instead as I was sorry I had ruined his life. Again he simply stared at me. I panicked and ran down the hall as I couldn't just stand there. I ran in and told Christopher, and he locked the door and held me. He said to just sit it out as there wasn't anything I could do.

Ten minutes went by, then twenty, then thirty. Finally we unlocked the door and quietly walked out. We could hear dishes clanging in the kitchen. We walked to the kitchen and, sure enough, Kerry was doing the dishes as if nothing had ever happened. I felt I was going crazy. What was wrong with him? Why would he do this to me? How can someone hate me so much?

I had contemplated killing myself numerous times. I felt God would certainly forgive me of my sins if I took my own life, but how? I didn't like guns and didn't want to feel that kind of pain, so I finally settled in on taking an overdose of Kerry's pills. So what if he realized I used his pills? At least he would be rid of me and I wouldn't have to perform anymore sex deeds for Christopher. This was perfect.

Then the reality set in; how would I face my parents in Heaven? They would be so disappointed in me and Christopher and our relationship which resulted in their death. Out of fear of seeing them again, I realized I couldn't kill myself, so I had to continue living in the hell I was currently living in and had to pray that in January my life would get better.

Before the end of the summer, Kerry came to me and told me he was selling our parents' house. I asked him why and he said he was ready to move on. Where would I go when I wanted to come home from college? He indicated clearly that wasn't his concern. I asked where I would live until I moved to A&M, and he replied that I could live with him, but if I chose to do that, all the furniture and everything would become his or I could find my own place and move out. If I did that, he would allow me to take what was in my bedroom—the choice was mine.

The next day I went to an apartment complex nearby, lied about my age, and was able to secure an apartment. For the next couple of days, I took various items and hid them in my closet, in my dresser, and under my mattress. I took pots and pans, silverware, towels, sheets and blankets, only things that I thought Kerry wouldn't readily miss. I couldn't believe he was going to take all my parents' belongings along with Ronnie's and basically kick me out.

I called my aunt and uncle and asked if they would come down the following weekend and help me move. They agreed so my aunt, uncle, Christopher, and I moved my bedroom furniture and clothes over to my new apartment. Kerry reluctantly agreed to give me Ronnie's couch and kitchen table only because he didn't want some of Ronnie's stuff but that was all I could have.

My aunt helped me get settled into my apartment. We had three dogs at the time, and since I was going to live in an apartment where dogs were not allowed, I had to find homes for two of my dogs. My small dog, Coco, I took with me as I figured I could hide him and the apartment management wouldn't know. He was a birthday present from my dad, so I had a special attachment to him. He had also flown to A&M with us on that fateful weekend and came home with me so I was especially close to him.

Once everything was finally in place at my apartment, I had a moment alone with my aunt. I started crying. I told her I was scared. I didn't want to stay there by myself. I already wanted to go home. She explained that I had no choice and this was a good idea for me, especially since things weren't working out between Kerry and me. Maybe this would stop some of the arguments. I asked her to spend the night with me, but she indicated it was a long drive home and she and my uncle needed to leave. That night I cried myself to sleep.

I hated living in an apartment. This was an adult world and I was still a teenager. I had a small Social Security check, which I now finally received. Kerry had received it prior to my moving into an apartment. I am not sure what he spent it on, but at least I had this to live on, plus the $10,000 from Ronnie's insurance policy that I would use to help me through college. I didn't need a lot of money as I wasn't eating very much, and I only went to school so there were utilities, gas, and insurance for my car and the apartment rent, so I did okay. Going to school every day, I had to pass through my parents' neighborhood, and each morning tears welled up in my eyes as I passed our street.

Finally one Saturday one of my friends came by to see my apartment. I was elated to have someone over. We talked for the longest time, and at some point we started talking about Christopher. I was finally ready to share some of my sorrow with someone I felt I could confide in. I was explaining to her I wasn't very happy and that Christopher was controlling. We had only been talking about him for maybe ten or fifteen minutes when there was a knock on the door. I looked out the peephole and it was Christopher! She quickly picked up her purse and left.

Christopher asked what we were talking about and I

said just girl stuff. Little did I know, as he walked up to my door, he could hear us talking. I didn't realize the walls were thin enough that anyone could hear us. He had stood outside the door and had heard everything I had said. He was furious with me. The very idea that I would be talking about him and his relationship with me to someone else!

He started yelling at me and telling me that we were through. He hoped I understood that no one else would put up with me, and I would spend a miserable life by myself. I cried out to please forgive me as I didn't mean to say anything that would make him mad. He asked for his promise ring back and I refused. He threw me onto the couch and almost broke my finger getting the ring off. Then he left. I lay on the couch and cried, wondering what had I done. Now I have no one in my life, I am truly all alone. Being alone was my biggest fear as the world seemed so big to me. Who would I talk to?

A few hours later Christopher returned. He had calmed down and gave me back the ring, but made me promise I wouldn't talk about him to anyone else ever again or he would be gone. I promised and I kept that promise for way too many years.

November 18, 1977 (I turned eighteen on the seventeenth of November) was my last day of high school and was also the date that my parents' house sold. A few months earlier I had hired an attorney trying to stop the sale of the house, but Kerry blocked the hiring of the attorney as at the time I had hired this man I was only seventeen, so legally I couldn't hire an attorney. Now I just surrendered and simply signed the selling documents so Kerry could have what he wanted.

I was tired of the fighting and I just wanted to move on with my new life at college. I was now considered an adult, so I couldn't be threatened to be sent away to an orphanage ever again or forced to take drugs I didn't want to take. I could cry if I wanted to and have pictures of my family out.

At the same time, I could never go home again, as my family's home now belonged to someone else. I told myself things would be better once I started college. There would be new friends and new things to do. Little did I know that it would still be a long time before I didn't feel like the "lonely me." Moving to A&M wasn't going to change anything for me as my pain was moving with me.

CHAPTER 9
Away at College

"Everything hurts."
Michelangelo

I guess every girl wants to live a fairy tale life. For me, going away to college was going to be my long awaited fairy tale, but I suppose I hadn't given too much realistic thought to the idea. First I was going to be in College Station, the place where my family died. Then I was going to live in the trailer my father had bought for my brother and me to live in while going to college. This was the last place I had any memories of my family. I hadn't thought about the toll this would take on me emotionally.

The flip side of the coin was I wouldn't be so accessible to Christopher anymore so I could have some breathing room, and I thought being in a new place and around new people, I could possibly make some new friends who wouldn't judge me as they wouldn't know about my past.

I had only lived in the trailer about a week when

Living Through The Pain

Kerry told me what my monthly rental payment to him would be. I couldn't believe he would ask me for rent! He said if I wasn't living there, we would sell the trailer and he could have his half of the money. I asked him what he thought his half was worth and he said $6,500. So instead of paying him monthly rent, I took part of Ronnie's insurance money and paid him off. There was no sister/brother relationship anymore as everything was strictly business between us.

Originally I had been accepted to A&M with a declared major in Marine Biology. Christopher put a quick stop to that way of thinking. He told me that wasn't a degree for a girl and directed me to switch over to Business, which was more appropriate. I don't know why I was so easily swayed by him. I don't know if I felt I had to allow his controlling nature for me to stay his girlfriend or if he had become some sort of father image for me, so I trusted his guidance. Regardless, I passed up my dream and quickly changed my major to Business (Finance) and hated it.

The transition was hard. The campus was huge and I was so timid. Everything was different. The classes were much harder than I had thought they would be and there was so much studying that needed to be done. My ability to concentrate had greatly been compromised based upon my life experiences thus far. I quickly got overwhelmed. I bit off a little too much too soon. Besides, the last one and a half years of my life had been pretty traumatic, I hadn't even processed all of that, and now here I was at college.

I was in over my head. I was taking sixteen hours and not doing very well in any of my classes considering I had the expectation I would be making A's. I had a History class where my first exam I made an "F", then in Economics my first exam I made a "D'. In Economics there was this cute guy who set next to me and he said he would be willing to tutor me. I could tell he liked me, but I was so gun shy because of Christopher that I decided to drop that class. This allowed me to focus on History bringing my overall grade up to a "C". At the end of that semester I was disappointed in myself as I had accumulated thirteen hours with three "B"s and two "C"s.

My first semester was pretty typical as it would have been for anyone. The only exception is I had no friends. Since I wasn't in a dormitory and I was extremely shy, I found myself becoming even more introverted. I would go home on weekends to visit Christopher and stay at Kerry's house. The condition of staying there is that I would be his maid over the weekend to earn my keep, so as soon as I got there on Friday afternoon, I would do the clothes, wash the dishes, vacuum, and clean his house; then I had the rest of the weekend to be with Christopher.

Then there were football weekends, which I absolutely loved! There was always a Friday night concert, midnight yell practice, then the game on Saturday afternoon. These were the weekends when I felt like a typical college kid and I was able to forget all my problems with the world and really enjoy life and live a little.

Toward the end of my first year in college, I started receiving phone calls late at night. They were collect calls from a woman named Curtis (my mother's name). This lady would cry and scream on the phone saying she was in

Dallas and why wouldn't I come get her. How could we have just left them in that cold and wet field?

At first I panicked and tried talking to the lady and realized it wasn't my mom, but after she hung up, I wondered would I really remember what my mom sounded like? Could this really be her? As the late night phone calls continued, I finally had my phone number changed as I couldn't handle such horrible episodes. I always wondered if this was my brother having someone terrorize me as I wouldn't have put it past him, he was so cruel to me.

At times while visiting Kerry, he would tell me he was going to sell some of my parents' furniture in a garage sale, but he always gave me first dibs. As usual, I couldn't stand the prospect of any of my family's furnishings going away, so I always bought them from Kerry at what seemed like top dollar to me, but Kerry was willing to negotiate on the price. Little by little I got part of my family's furnishings back, and it helped me transform my trailer into a place that felt like home. I felt I had my family closer to me by having their things, familiar things, in my life again.

I had hopes of having numerous friends while attending college; however, Christopher had different ideas about that. He didn't like the idea of me having contact with anyone else, I think because he was fearful he might lose his hold on me. Nevertheless, I always tried to follow his direction and guidance, so I never went out of my way to have any friends or to do anything.

There were three single guys living in the trailer next to me. Jackson was about one year ahead of me in college and majoring in Finance as well. He was just a nice guy. He never made any moves on me as he understood I was attached at the hips to Christopher. One afternoon, though, he stopped by and invited me to go to the basketball game with him and his brother. I think it was more of a way of getting me out as he saw how much of a hermit I was. I wanted to go, but knew Christopher wouldn't approve so I declined. Stupidly, I mentioned it to Christopher. The next time Christopher came to visit me, he went directly to Jackson's, knocked on the door, and when Jackson answered, Christopher pushed him hard against the door and threatened him to leave me alone. I was so embarrassed.

After that incident, Christopher would periodically just show up at the trailer unannounced. He came one time when I had gone to stroll the mall and window shop as I didn't want to go home. He quickly put a stop to that as well. It was clear, I was only to go to school, the grocery store, and home—no place else. Once again I felt like a prisoner.

I never knew how to simply take it easy, so when summertime rolled around I enrolled in summer school in Houston. Being busy studying prevented me from having a wandering mind, which could easily have led to severe depression. I lived with Kerry and went to Community College, taking twelve hours that summer.

At the end of summer, Kerry decided he was going to sell his townhouse and move. He had a Chevy Blazer that he had just gotten new tires installed on and had the brakes fixed, and he offered for me to use it to move anything that I wanted in his house that he was leaving behind. I quickly took him up on his offer as he had never been this generous before and it didn't cost me any money.

The Fall Semester started and Kerry no longer offered me the same arrangement in his new house. I had a friend of Ronnie's (actually an old girlfriend, Debra) who agreed to let me stay at her apartment on the weekends. This was great as she was a nice person and someone who could be my friend.

I was about two or three weeks into the new semester when I was home for the weekend and at Christopher's parents' house. We had just finished dinner when the doorbell rang. Christopher's dad answered the door and I heard him say yes, Christopher and Cathy are here, just a minute. We both came to the door and the man indicated he was a process server. Needless to say, I was stunned. I couldn't imagine what this was about. We sat down and read the documents.

Kerry was suing both of us for stealing his property! He listed enough stuff that it was well over $500, so if convicted it would be a felony. You can imagine how I felt. I wanted to crawl under their table and not be seen. Now I was bringing legal problems into their home! Christopher's dad was furious and I understood but I had nothing to do with it. It all went back to Kerry graciously offering up the remaining furnishings at his house and these were the items he listed in his lawsuit.

I had to hire someone to represent us as this was pretty serious. The attorney couldn't believe that my brother was suing over family property that was to be divided equally between us. Not only that, but on Monday morning a Sheriff's Officer came into my classroom. He showed a document to the professor and the professor called my name out. Kerry was also having me served at school! I was so humiliated.

That night I got a call from my college advisor asking questions about being served at school by the Sheriff's Department. I told him it was a family problem. There had been a big misunderstanding between my brother and myself. He advised that if I got into trouble with the law, I could be expelled. I assured him I had done nothing wrong.

Every weekend I called my mom's parents. We talked about various things, mainly how I was doing and how they were doing. This particular weekend Kerry was visiting them, and he got on the phone with me before I spoke to my Grandpa. It was on this phone call that he told me he was a homosexual. I couldn't believe this on top of everything else! I scolded him and yelled back that I was tired of him playing games with me. I wasn't going to put up with it any longer. He said it was the truth and he had been this way since junior high, but he had kept it a secret. I didn't believe him. What would my parents say?

We argued for a few more minutes and then I hung up. I never called back as I knew my grandparents hated us arguing as we were all each other had. They would want to know what we were arguing about and I knew I couldn't tell them. The following week my Grandpa died of a heart attack while in the bathroom shaving. I never got to talk to my Grandpa and tell him that I loved him like I always had done as I had hung up the phone. The last he knew, Kerry and I were arguing. I felt shameful once again, and now there would be another funeral to go to.

Living Through The Pain

As the months rolled by there always seemed to be something horrific happening. I am not sure I would have known how to handle just an average life anymore. The lawsuit my brother had against Christopher and me was settled before a judge. He scolded my brother, indicating that this suit should have never been filed as how could he possibly rule on furnishings that were inherited by us both equally, so the case was dismissed.

Next there was the contact letter from the IRS indicating that I owed taxes on the sale of my parents' house. Kerry had filed the paperwork using my Social Security number. The estate hadn't even settled, so I didn't have any funds to claim, but I was nevertheless worried as I knew no one wanted trouble with the IRS. Again the attorney helped me and that was cleared up.

That Christmas, Christopher and I became engaged. I was now hopeful that I might have a normal life. Marrying him probably would mean that God would forgive me of my sins and so would my parents because all the sexual escapades had been with him and if ultimately he became my husband, then certainly that would wipe that debt away. It made perfect sense to me. This was my way out. I was bargaining with God to ease my guilt.

By the time I got ready to start back for the Spring Semester, Debra asked if she could move in with me as she wanted to go back to school and work on her Master's. I didn't know what to say as I was so used to living by myself, but I felt I owed her that much. Christopher was adamantly opposed to it. He said she would steer me away from my studies and would make concentrating hard for me. I ultimately told her no, but looking back I realize Christopher didn't want me to get too close to anyone. If given the opportunity to have someone befriend me, I would probably have ultimately confided in that person and would have found the strength to break up with Christopher, but the path I took didn't allow me access to a friend.

By chance I found out that my father had a $100,000 life insurance that my brother had never mentioned. As I began processing things in my brain, I started realizing that Kerry and the Executor of my parents' estate had been pretty cozy, and it seemed like Kerry was living a much higher lifestyle than I. There was the prior Christmas where he spent the entire month of December in Austria, then he seemed to travel to Europe a lot and every year he bought a new car. I began to think, someone was skimming money from the estates.

Oddly enough thinking back, a few months before the accident, my parents had both sat me down and had a serious talk with me. They wanted to know who I would want in charge of their Estate if something happened to the both of them. That was a strange and ominous statement. I told them Ronnie, of course, but they pushed a little further. They didn't want any of the kids over the Estate to prevent bickering. I asked them what was this all about? They simply told me they were getting their wills in order and wanted to know my thoughts.

I mentioned my dad's longtime business partner, Ed, as he was the only other person I knew. Little did I know they ultimately chose Ed as the Independent Executor. Well, Kerry and Ed began to work their magic to take as much of my inheritance as they could get by with or least that was my opinion.

In one of my classes at A&M, I met a girl whose father was an attorney in Houston. I set up an appointment with him. He and his partner took my case. I was relieved that they didn't think I was crazy as I have to admit my story was bizarre. Little did I know that the case would go on until mid–1984.

Shortly after hiring the attorneys, my brother filed a petition in East Texas to split my parents' ranch. I hated this idea as the ranch needed to remain in one piece. Here was yet another case that needed to be handled. After several months of brief filings and hearings, the judge ruled that the property couldn't be split as it would have negative consequences on the value of the property. For now at least I had won the case and bought myself some much needed time with my brother.

I have to say I was exhausted. Life was hard for me. I never had time to relax, and I always felt I had to be on guard, ready for the next shoe to drop at any moment. There was no one who could predict what would be happening to me next. I realized that Christopher was right; who would ever want me but him? Talk about baggage, I had more than anyone else could possibly have.

I don't know how I remained sane. I didn't go to church. I had tried several times, but as soon as I started hearing songs that I remembered from my childhood, I would break down. Also going to church meant I had to be humble and face my shame, which I just couldn't do. I prayed off and on, but nothing consistently. I simply survived day by day. If it wasn't for the constant demand of school, I think I would have gone crazy as this gave my mind something else to focus on.

By now Ronnie's estate had settled and I had gotten about $32,000. I invested the funds in a certificate of deposit to insure I wouldn't go out and spend the money on something foolish. Besides, this was all I had to fall back on.

The following summer I took twenty-four hours to ensure I could graduate early. Both my dad and Ronnie had graduated from A&M in three years, and I was determined to graduate in two and half years. I think I was always finding ways to push myself so I wouldn't have to face the reality of my true emotional state. I was afraid if I did, I would have a nervous breakdown, so I did what I knew best, and that was school. Ultimately when I graduated in August of 1980, I did so with only a GPA of 2.73. I had wanted to graduate with honors, so I was disappointed in myself, but I did successfully graduate and I told myself that was the main thing.

I graduated on August 16, 1980 and got married on August 29, 1980. So while going to school, I planned (and paid for) the wedding. In addition, Christopher and I wanted to live in a house when we got married. By this time in my life, I had decided all I wanted was a house, kids, a dog (which I still had Coco), and somehow my life would be perfect—I would be normal again.

Christopher's dad found us a new home in a small community right outside of Houston. The house was perfect. I had gotten about $60,000 now from my parents' estate, and I took $50,000 and used it as the down payment on the house. Christopher and I had a verbal agreement that this would protect the $50,000 from ever being used and, once we had children and they graduated from college, we could pull this money out and divide it among our kids as a gift from the grandparents they never knew. This seemed like the best business thing to do as it would help us buy our first home. In time, I found that Christopher wouldn't honor this agreement.

CHAPTER 10
The Wedding and Honeymoon

> "To love means loving the unlovable.
> To forgive means pardoning the unpardonable.
> Faith means believing the unbelievable. Hope means
> hoping when everything else seems hopeless."
>
> G.K. Chesterton

The night before the wedding, one of my bridesmaids spent the night with me. She tried to convince me not to marry Christopher. She felt he was too controlling and I still had time to stop the wedding. My attorneys had also tried to convince me not to marry Christopher, but if I was set on it, then at least I should have a prenuptial in place. I refused as why would I be getting married if I didn't trust Christopher?

I did trust him, but I also knew I shouldn't be getting married. The morning of the wedding, my friend and I went to the mall so I could have a professional apply my makeup. Christopher had specifically told me not to use blue eye shadow. Well, of course, what did the makeup artist use but blue as she thought it would accent my blue eyes nicely. I thought I looked rather pretty so I didn't think much about it.

When I began to walk down the aisle, I was nervous. Actually I wanted to run, but I was too scared to. I really didn't want to get married, and I didn't know what to do. The family friend who was walking me down the aisle started telling me jokes to cheer me up. I had invited Kerry to come to the wedding. After all, he was the only true family I had even if he was a rat bastard.

As I walked slowly down the aisle, I didn't see him. I was deeply hurt, but knowing the problems we had had, I understood why he wouldn't want to be there. It wasn't until many, many years later that I truly regretted not asking him to give me away. I should have been a bigger person as he was my brother and I loved him. It would have been appropriate for him to give me away, but with the ongoing feuds between us, I honestly never thought of it.

The ceremony was beautiful and everything went according to plan. When I turned around, there was Kerry sitting in the back of the room. I was elated! My heart was pounding in my chest as my brother had indeed come to my wedding. What a joyous sight! We had our pictures made, ate cake, and greeted our guests. Kerry wished us well, then left. Again, I felt alone as I missed my mom and dad not being there. I knew in my heart if they were alive, I wouldn't have married Christopher, but that was the past, so I needed to focus on my future.

Christopher and I went to change clothes. I made the mistake of asking if I had looked alright as Christopher never said I looked beautiful. Every bride wants her groom to tell her she looks beautiful. He indicated I looked alright, why? I told him about my eye shadow and, when he realized I had blue on, he started yelling at me! He yelled, "Can't you follow one simple instruction I give you?" I was devastated and my heart sank all the way down into my stomach. I was now a much stronger woman, so I didn't cry. I simply changed clothes and we left the church.

That night while Christopher slept beside me, I quietly cried to my mom. I knew even if she was still mad at me for the premarital sex, she would understand how miserable I was and how I felt trapped. I was now married, but I knew I didn't love Christopher; I just wanted to get rid of the guilt and shame I had carried all of these years. Oh, how I wish there had been someone I could have talked to. The next morning we left for our honeymoon in Hawaii.

I had previously been to Hawaii with my parents, yet somehow every visit it always seems like a new place and quite magical. The tropical breeze, beautiful scenery, and awesome sunsets are a delight for all who visit the Islands. I was determined that I would turn out to be a good wife to Christopher and make this marriage work beginning with our honeymoon.

Our honeymoon lasted two weeks. We vacationed in Oahu, Maui, Kauai, and the big island of Hawaii, then came back to Los Angeles and went to Disneyland before heading back to Houston. It was a wonderful vacation, and I was so ready for some relaxing fun away from all of my personal problems. I think for the most part we did the typical touristy things along with a lot of sightseeing.

For me there were two incidents which come to mind which foretold what our marriage would really be like. The first incident happened when we went snorkeling. One morning we drove to Hanauma Bay on the island of Oahu. At this spot a person could snorkel out beyond the reef following the cables for safety. However, extreme caution is required so as not to get pulled into the reef by the waves which are dangerous, and the coral is extremely sharp.

I have always been a good swimmer, just not a strong swimmer, and the waves and current were extremely strong that day. Christopher indicated not to be worried as he would swim along the side of me. Well, as soon as we got close to the reef, he went off and left me right at the time I started experiencing trouble. I ended up with a charley horse in my leg, and I couldn't kick hard enough to stay away from the reef. The waves caught me and pounded me into the coral. I could immediately feel pain in my leg. I was struggling to stay away from the coral and was yelling for help.

A lifeguard on the beach swam out and pulled me to safety. My leg had received a horrible gash. He placed a tourniquet on my leg and kept me lying down on the beach until finally Christopher returned. The lifeguard said I should go to the hospital to have stitches. Of course we never went to the hospital. Christopher's idea was I needed Band-Aids and to go into the salt water periodically to keep the wound clean and prevent infection.

Toward the end of our trip, we went to Kauai. We stayed at the Coco Palms. There were tall, luscious green coconut trees (actually a coconut grove) surrounding the hotel. The hotel was famous as Elvis Presley filmed *Blue Hawaii* there in 1961. There was an exquisite and romantic restaurant on the property. Christopher made reservations for us.

The dining room was dimly lit. I remember tropical birds in cages throughout the restaurant. Where we were sitting, I don't recall anyone else sitting near us. Once we ordered our meal, Christopher decided he wanted oral sex, right there. He was persistent, so I had no choice but to crawl under the table in my cocktail dress, unzip his pants, and do the deed. It was humiliating, and I quickly lost my appetite. I was so embarrassed and felt so ashamed of what I had become. That night I slept on the floor in front of the door crying. He never even asked me why I wouldn't come to bed; maybe he didn't care at all.

Regardless, I was the trouper and I found a way to survive yet again. When we finally returned to Houston, I was more determined than ever to make our marriage work, and I knew I could do this. I just needed to get a different mindset and be positive. In time it would all work out. At least that is what I told myself. Time would eventually prove me wrong again.

CHAPTER 11

1980–1985

"When we are desperate, God can do His greatest work."
Author Unknown

I have given a great deal of thought about this chapter of the book. There is so much to tell that only a woman would appreciate and empathize with me in regard to the turmoil and abuse (mental and sexual, not physical) I suffered, yet I feel I must remain silent. I do so for two important reasons: (1) this information would not be beneficial for my son to know and could possibly damage his relationship with his father, which is not the intent of my book, and (2) I do believe that what happens behind closed doors between a husband and a wife is sacred and should not be shared lightly with others.

What I feel is valid to state is that the relationship I had with Christopher prior to our marriage only continued to deteriorate once we were married. The reality is I was damaged goods from the beginning due to our first sexual encounter that should have never happened, and in combining that with the timing of the accident made me a different type of woman; one that I wouldn't have normally turned out to be. That doesn't mean Christopher isn't responsible for his actions, as he is, but he was a young man with great sexual desires and he had an easy target with me, so he took advantage of that situation.

In other words it does take "two to tango." If I could have found the courage, (which I should have), if only I would had gone to counseling to understand sexual relationships, (which I didn't), if I only would have spoken to a pastor or counselor or even a friend about my guilt, shame, and sin, (which I was too scared to do), I could have stepped away from Christopher. The entire circumstances we both were in allowed for the destructive behavior to continue. We each played our unique roles, and as a victim, I felt trapped. Christopher hurt me in ways he still doesn't fully understand to this very day and, quite frankly, he doesn't care.

I know when I filed for divorce, it took Christopher by surprise and he was hurt. He did definitely take advantage of a young naïve teenage girl, but a lot of guys do that. He should get credit for helping me through the toughest time when losing my family. He didn't truly understand my pain, but how could he? Yet I know I wasn't an easy person to be around with all my problems.

So for any woman out there who is suffering, only you can end your suffering. Take responsibility for your situation and get out and move on with your life. Get counseling, talk to someone. The worst thing for everyone involved is to stay in a relationship out of fear, confusion, shame, or guilt. You are stronger than you give yourself credit for. Also, an important saying by an unknown author is so true, "When God solves your problems, you have faith in his abilities; when God doesn't solve your problems, He has faith in your abilities." So have faith in yourself and remember God loves you regardless of any sin you commit, so don't punish yourself like I did. I still had many, many more lessons to learn in life before I found my peace.

CHAPTER 12

The Affair That Ended the Marriage

"Oh, that he would kiss me with the kisses of his mouth! For your love is more delightful than wine."

Song of Songs 1:1–2

The Texas economy hit rock bottom in the mid-eighties. Oil and real estate had taken a dive and I found myself laid off from work. Instead of seeing this as a blessing, I felt more of a panic as I was the main bread earner in the family. I should have taken this time to relax, enjoy being a mom, and settle in to staying at home for a while. The reality was we couldn't afford this. I was unemployed for about three months when I got an interview with a company that did wholesale travel packages. At the time I accepted the job, I had also decided to go back to school and obtain my master's degree.

Not long on the job I realized the company was having huge financial problems. As I began to peel back the finances of the business, the more apparent it became that one of the partners was embezzling money from the business. With any amount of common sense, I should have quit the job, but instead I saw it more of a challenge to see if I could turn the company around.

At the same time, I would hear about the various trips that the staff would take from time to time to check out properties, and invariably there were tales of affairs, drinking, partying, and plain living it up. This was foreign to me, something I wasn't interested in, so I kept my head down, focused on the company finances, and continued going to school at night.

It was December 1985. My boss, Carl, suggested that I should go with the company on a weekend trip to Acapulco. Acapulco sounded so exciting! I was scared to think about it, but I really wanted to go and see what the world had to offer me. I went home and discussed it with Christopher. He was adamant that I couldn't go, especially after all the stories I had told him.

Nevertheless, a voice spoke up from inside me, and I said I was going and he couldn't make me change my mind. I clearly remember the "deer in the headlights" look from him as he stood there dazed at what I had said. I could hardly believe it myself, but I stood my ground and he backed down. He voiced his concerns, and deep inside I knew he was right that I shouldn't be going. Nick was only a little over a year old. What could I possibly be thinking of, yet I kept thinking about it and couldn't say no.

When the plane took off, I couldn't believe I was actually on board and going away for some fun. I planned on taking it all in as I probably would never do something crazy like this again. When we exited the plane, the warm tropical breeze was intoxicating to me. All our rooms looked out over the ocean. I couldn't believe how beautiful it was and that I was really there. We spent the remainder of the day touring some select properties. After dinner, everyone decided to go to one of the local discos.

I had never been to a disco before. The sound of the music bounced off my body. The strobe lights, the tequila, the laughter, the dancing and sweating; I felt alive! I was more like a kid in a candy story. Here I was twenty–six years old and had never been to a disco or club! We partied for several hours when I finally said I had had enough and needed to go to my room and lie down. Carl said it wasn't safe for a young woman to walk back to the hotel by herself, so he accompanied me.

The cool ocean breeze felt good on my skin and, being away from the lights and noise, I slowly began to come back down to Earth. We strolled along and talked and laughed, and it was enjoyable for me. When we arrived back at my room, Carl asked if he could come in and check out the view from my balcony. I said yes and we strolled to the balcony and gazed at the stars and moon. It had been a perfect evening. I had had so much fun. As I walked him back to the door, he stopped, pulled me close and kissed me passionately. He slowly started to unbutton my dress when I stopped him. I told him I couldn't, I was married. I told him I wantedt to and, if I could, I would with him, but I couldn't. He left.

As the door closed behind him, all I could hear was

the echo from the door closing, then silence. I stood there for the longest time. Wow—he just kissed me! He must think I am special. It felt good. How stupid I must have sounded, "I would if I could." I just blew my only chance of ever being with someone else to see what it was like. Wow, he kissed me!

I was like a teenager again. I couldn't sleep all night. I had butterflies in my stomach. Oh, to just be held where I felt like a woman, like someone who was desirable and sensual.

The next day was awkward as I didn't know how to act. I felt like I was special to him and wondered if others could tell. I didn't pay any attention to the properties we visited; all I could think about was him. What would I do if I had the chance again? Would I be able to go through with it? Would he try to make a move again or had he respected what I had said? Maybe I could make a move? Oh, if he would just kiss me again so I could have that feeling just one more time.

Well, I got the chance as that night repeated itself. We started at the disco and worked up a fierce sweat. We would brush up against each other, and it felt like electricity shooting through my veins. As the night wore on, he asked if I was ready to go back to the hotel and I said yes. I wondered if he would ask to come inside again. Should I invite him? This is my last night, what do I do?

We reached my room; I told him good night, opened the door, and he stepped in right behind me. I never even had a chance to turn the lights on. He gently unbuttoned my clothes and slowly moved me to the bed where he caressed me as I gently fell backwards onto the pillow. His kisses were like sweet honey to my lips. He caressed my breasts, then slid on top of me. There was no resistance on my part as my body willingly wrapped around his. I began to tremble inside and began to feel what felt like an explosion of senses, only to realize this was my first organism! That was one of many for that night as we made love seven times before the sun came up.

I so hated for the morning sun to break the sky as it meant my dream had come to an end. He gently brushed my hair out of my face, tenderly kissed my lips and then he was gone.

He was fifteen years my senior, golden brown hair, beautiful brown eyes; not the kind of guy I ever thought I would go for, but then did I even have a clue what my type was? Oh he smelled so good. I didn't even care that he was married. I had never felt like this before.

Guilt? I felt no guilt. All I felt was the tingle he had left me with and an amazement of how womanly I felt. I had changed that night as I had become a woman. He treated me like a woman as he gently made love to me. I can only equate it to what I hear about cocaine; once you take a hit, you are addicted. Well, I was addicted to making love, not having sex. What would I do now? How would I return to the life I had? Would Christopher figure it out? Would I be able to hide this most wonderful, sensuous experience from him? Would he be able to sense the difference in me?

When I arrived back in Houston, I couldn't make eye contact with Christopher. Yes, he definitely knew something was a foul. I didn't know then, but everything had changed for me. I had literally transformed into someone else, and there was no going back. Life as I had known it with my husband was over for good. I had found my womanly strength to stand up for myself. I now knew what it felt like to be a woman. I knew what it felt like to have someone make love to me. I knew what intimacy felt like, what tenderness felt like. Yes, I had changed; the world had become crystal clear to me, and I knew what I hungered for. I didn't have to be abused any longer.

CHAPTER 13
The Hunger

"When you try to fill an unholy hunger, you are never satisfied, your hunger only grows. But when you finally fill your unholy hunger through atonement, your longing is no more."

Cathy Kurtz

I became obsessed with making love to Carl. We would sneak out at lunch. I would stay late at work. We would meet up in the parking lot. I didn't care where or how daring it was, I couldn't say no, and every time we made love, I wanted more. My body literally ached to be loved.

Christopher would try to get close to me, but I would push him away. He knew, because he never tried to be demanding anymore. He bought me gifts, told me how pretty I was, sent me flowers. Nothing mattered anymore. I could only envision being with Carl and having my son and not having to deal with Christopher anymore.

Living Through The Pain

By February I had gone to a therapist. The therapist listened to what I had to say and this is what she said, "Close your eyes and now imagine yourself being trapped in a dark, cold, scary cave. You were led to believe this was all there was to life and you accepted that; but one day, someone came along and rolled the stone away, and you could see light for the first time. You carefully took your first step out of the cave and you saw the beautiful blue sky. You saw the lush green grass and you could smell the perfume of the flowers. You could hear the sweet sound of birds as they sang, and you could feel the cool breeze on your cheeks. Then your husband comes back and scolds you and tells you, you must go back into the cave as that is all that there is for you. However, what you have seen is so stimulating, you can't go back and you won't. To do so is to give up your life and your happiness." She said she never had advised anyone to get a divorce before, but I was her exception.

With that in mind, I hired an attorney and filed for divorce. I wouldn't have thought Christopher would have fought me, but he did. I don't think he fought for me as much as he fought for what I could provide for him. His parents also pushed him to fight for their grandchild. Going into the divorce I had three strikes against me: (1) I didn't have a tough attorney; (2) I was hiding my affair; and (3) and my life wasn't right with God.

CHAPTER 14
The Struggle to Press On

"Most of the important things accomplished in the world have been accomplished by people who have kept on trying when there seemed to be no hope at all."

Dale Carnegie

My attorney, I thought, was a bull dog, which is what I needed. He was more old-school, yet I felt he was actually making side deals behind my back with the opposing counsel. Even though I didn't have much money, there was $50,000 worth of equity which I put down on the house and then there was my parents' farm in East Texas. I owned half of it out right and had purchased the other half from my brother and was in debt trying to pay off the loan. My attorney had no problems telling me he would like to own my father's farm. I knew at least I had collateral for an attorney so I kept him.

I wrongly assumed that Christopher would be respectful regarding the divorce and would move out of the house, especially since I provided the down payment for the house and I was the main wage earner. I couldn't have been more wrong. He adamantly refused to leave the house. I was forced to move upstairs and continue to live in a house with him, which was a horrible way to live.

He watched my every move. I had to lay towels down on the floor to block the crack under the doorway when I took a shower. I felt like a prisoner in my own home. He would go through my clothes, my drawers, my purses, and even my car; I suppose trying to find out why I wanted a divorce. In all actuality, he just needed to look inward to the type of man he was and how I had been treated to find his answer.

Several months into this new way of living, I woke up and heard noises from downstairs. His mother, father, sister, and brother-in-law were all in my house moving things out as quickly as they could into a moving trailer. I tried to stop them, but with five people, I couldn't control the situation. I should have called the police, but I didn't. I saw stuff leaving that had belonged to my parents and it broke my heart. I felt like I was being robbed by people who supposedly cared about me and my son. Christopher wanted his half of everything, even down to the kitchen spices, which he split into baggies.

When I spoke to my attorney, all he indicated was that Christopher must have realized it was close to the time the judge was going to force him out, so he grabbed everything he could. As they say, "possession is nine–tenths of the law" and my attorney indicated he was going to be able to keep everything he had taken. Unfortunately, it didn't stop there.

They then went to my parents' farm and took tools and supplies. I felt at that point like I had been raped as this now was personal.

Christopher finally moved out of the house and I could breathe again. I kept my affair with Carl under wraps as I hadn't been raised this way, and I felt tremendous guilt about what I was doing and even more so that I was enjoying it. We were careful when we got together to ensure no one would see us. I actually lived for those few personal and intimate moments of being wanted and needed.

The judge made it as difficult as he could on me when he scheduled visitation. The judge temporarily ruled that Christopher got our son every Wednesday night and three weekends out of the month. I was going to graduate school at night, so it made it difficult for me to see my son since I had only one weekend to enjoy my son and the evenings I had to study once I got him to bed. The judge scolded me by saying I needed to decide if I wanted to be a mom or a business professional. I was trying to get a solid education where I could support my son and ensure I could afford to pay for his college when the time came. Christopher never seemed to have a solid profession, so I had doubts that he would be able to support our son, so that meant it would fall on my shoulders. It seemed that the more I tried to get my life on track, the more I was punished.

Even with Christopher being out of the house, I felt victimized. His parents would constantly drive by, and I always felt I was being watched. I quickly realized this was not going to be the life I wanted, constantly being under the microscope of someone else. As a result, I decided to

Living Through The Pain

start looking for a job out-of-state. That was a scary thought for me, but I felt it was the only way my son and I would ever have a shot at a "normal" life. I also felt a start in a new state would help minimize my pain about my family as I would have no memories in a new location and no one would know of my father.

I focused on three states, California and Florida (for the beaches) and Colorado (for the mountains). I had never lived any place else, so I thought I could take comfort in either the ocean or the mountains for solitude and peace. Not too long into my job search, I ended up with two interviews with Disney (both in California). One was in Anaheim working for the travel company and the other was in Glendale working for the studio.

Looking back, I probably should have gone for the studio job, but I wanted to be close to the ocean and the Anaheim job allowed me to live in Corona del Mar. I accepted the offer, which included two months' rent and moving costs from Texas. I felt like I had hit the jackpot, at least until I spoke to my attorney.

He wasn't thrilled with the idea I was moving out-of-state while going through a custody battle. I told him my reasons and that this would give me a solid career. I was advised to leave my son behind until we could get something settled by the judge. This time I felt he was wrong. To leave my son, all my senses told me I would be accused of abandoning my baby. He said if I took him without the authority to do so, it would be considered kidnapping.

How did my life turn out this way? I prayed long and hard about it. I knew this was my chance to escape Texas, especially since Disney would pay for my move. I couldn't afford to move otherwise. I didn't even mind leaving Carl behind. What was important was starting over with Nick, having a solid career path, and being in a safe location with Nick away from his father. As risky as it was, I chose to move.

    Thursday morning, Christopher dropped off my son at the usual time. About thirty minutes later, the movers showed up and packed and moved all my stuff out of the house by 5 PM. Another moving trailer picked up my car, and I was set to fly out Friday morning to sunny California. I couldn't believe I had pulled this off so far.

    Friday morning arrived. I had my dog, Coco, crated for the flight and my son and I were on our way! As soon as I landed, I made two important calls from the airport; the first was to call Christopher to let him know where I was and my new address and, as soon as I got a phone number, I would provide it to him. Then I called my attorney and got yelled at. For once, I just smiled as I heard him curse me out. I was my own woman and I knew what was best for my son and me. After all, how could I be accused of kidnapping my son when everyone knows where we are, right?

    I quickly got settled into the little beach cottage I rented. Most of my stuff had to be stored as the cottage was so tiny. I went from an 1,800 square foot luxury home with a huge back yard to a tiny cottage so small I had to use an end table for a kitchen table. It made me think of the stories my mom and dad used to tell about when they first started out and literally had nothing. There is something quaint about nothing, just love. I had what I needed, my son and my peace of mind. For me, all was good with the world; at least so I thought.

CHAPTER 15
Slowly Unraveling

"It's time to let God's love cover all things in your life. All secrets. All hurts. All hours of evil, minutes of worry."

Max Lucado

Life was good. I got used to my new surroundings. I had a live-in au-pair from Germany who slept on the couch and took care of my son while I was at work during the day. I put my graduate studies on hold. I loved my new job at Disney, which was exciting and I was learning a lot. In the evening my son and I would walk to the beach and spend quality time together. There were many parks within walking distance for us to enjoy. I was at peace for the first time in a long time. I thought the worst was over, and then the dam broke and washed away all my dreams, my hope, and my strength.

My attorney called and informed me that the judge had ruled that my son would have to return to Texas every six weeks for a three week visitation! I was astonished. We had never been separated that long. How would he do and how would I do? I told him that was impossible and I wouldn't abide by such rules. He then informed me the judge anticipated that and had already written a warrant for my arrest should I fail to comply with his directives.

My world was shattered. I looked at my son's sweet little innocent face and wondered how my life could have gone so wrong that he would be punished this way. His dad volunteered to come out to get him. Little did I know this was so he could take pictures of my cottage for the divorce trial.

When he took my son out of my arms, it literally felt like my heart was being ripped out of my chest. Nick screamed, and I fell onto the ground crying as he drove my baby away. My world exploded. It was so quiet, all I could hear was the pounding of my heart and I could hardly breathe. I had no will to live. I barely ate, hardly slept, and was basically robotic at work. I had never known that kind of heartache before. It was so much worse than losing my family. This was my child whom I was supposed to protect, yet the judge had all the power over me.

Those three weeks felt like an eternity. When I got Nick back, he was different. He was introverted and moody. This once happy baby now cried every time I stepped away from him. He had difficulty sleeping. It was horrible. This arrangement went on until he started school at five. I couldn't imagine a judge being so cruel to a little baby. Most of the trips, I took off work on Friday afternoons and flew back with him to Houston, slept in the airport until the early Saturday morning flight, then flew back to

California, lonely, broken hearted, and severely depressed. Then three weeks later, I would return to pick him up. Nick's dad and grandparents rarely helped with the travel.

While all of this was going on, his dad decided my son needed an attorney, so his attorney forced the issue and of course, the judge awarded my son an attorney. I was accused of having a nervous breakdown with tendencies to be violent toward myself or Nick. There were no incidents to cite and I never got to defend myself against the allegations. As a result, the judge approved Christopher's motion and I was required to fly back to Houston for psychiatric testing. Just imagine the conversations I had to have with my new boss.

It seems no one understood why I moved or how I could even consider moving from Houston, my birth home. Even my aunts and uncles told me to come home. I thought that had to be laughable as they didn't want to help me as a sixteen–year–old, but now that I was a grown woman, they could tell me my decision was a bad one. I was not coming home. I had no home. I had neither family nor friends; there was only my son and me. I didn't want to live with someone always watching me or controlling me or my son, so 1,500 miles away from Houston looked pretty damn good to me. Besides, I had made a terrible choice in a husband and a father for my son; I certainly didn't want him influencing the way my baby grew up.

The battling over Nick and the divorce went on way too long. Christopher moved back into our home and utterly destroyed it. When he was finally removed from the home because the court sold the house, he had removed light fixtures, the microwave, door handles, toilets, you name it; if it was removable, he took it.

While he lived there, I was forced to pay the mortgage as I didn't want to ruin my credit, so he got to live there for free. I did shut off all the utilities, but that didn't matter. He used an Igloo as an ice chest and a camping lantern for lights at night. I hated that my son had to live this way, and the judge simply didn't care. As far as I was concerned this proved how little Christopher actually cared about his son. He was looking for a free ride and whatever assets he could take away from me. Worst of all, his parents supported him in this behavior.

Finally it was time for the trial. Nothing about my life ever was typical. When I arrived back in Houston, I found out that Texas allows a jury trial for custody battles, so naturally Christopher opted for a jury trial. It turned into a three and half week jury trial. I had to call my boss at Disney and explain. I was so embarrassed that I would have to be off for so long. Luckily he was an understanding man. I wasn't prepared to be gone that long. I didn't have very many clothes with me as originally I was told to expect about three days for the hearing. Luckily I had room on my credit card for the hotel, rental car, and food. I was so tight with my money that when my toothpaste ran out, I used soap for my toothbrush to brush my teeth. This was a low point in my life.

In addition I had kept up a lie for a long time. I never had admitted to the affair with Carl. During my depositions, I lied. That was my secret. I was ashamed at how far I had fallen in life, but the day before the trial began, I finally broke down and confessed to my attorney.

He was furious and indicated I might as was well hand over my son right now, as he felt there was no chance of me getting custody. He said how would the jury know if I was telling the truth now? I told him, if I got custody based on a lie, how would I live with myself and look at that precious boy and expect him to respect me? If I got custody of him, I had to do so honestly. I had nothing to gain by telling the truth except humiliation and possibly going to jail for perjuring myself, so of course I was now telling the truth. He told me I should have just kept lying. I cried for my mom's and dad's help, but I had no one in my corner. It seemed every decision I made only made my life worse.

I went back to my hotel room and wanted to kill myself. I couldn't let Nick be raised by his dad. How could I let him turn out just like him? I wanted more for my son. I wanted him to respect women, to be a Godly man; to be a family man and a successful family provider. I felt I had let my son down in so many ways, and he would never know the heartache I had experienced, how scary it was to file for divorce and make the ultimate decision to start my life over. What would I do?

I consoled myself that nothing else mattered. Between Kerry and Christopher, they had ruined my life. I wasn't going to let someone ruin Nick's life. Even though I was scared, I had to find the strength that if I lost custody, I had to be strong enough to take him and run away. I wasn't sure how or where; all I knew was that Nick deserved a shot at a normal life. I cried myself to sleep many nights in that lonely hotel room during the course of the trial. I had no one to talk to. All I had was God, and I wasn't sure He was even in my corner as I was so filled with guilt and shame, yet I prayed anyway.

CHAPTER 16
The Long Painful Trial

"When the way is long and you cannot see the path,
when you feel abandoned and all but forgotten,
hang on . . . the Lord is near."

Linda E. Knight

The trial lasted three and half weeks. My father had worked hard to have a stellar reputation in the community. I was raised in a Christian home and knew before the trial ever started that some of the testimony was going to be graphic and painful to tell. The details were things I wouldn't even share with my closest friend, yet here I found myself in front of twelve complete strangers.

The jurors all had listened to my dad on the radio and watched him on TV. There were reporters covering the trial and other curious people who were sitting in on the trial, and here I was having to share my most personal, private, intimate, sickening details of my life with Christopher, then talk about the affair. My parents would be so disappointed in me. I was disappointed in myself and sickened at the thought of what was going to happen.

I don't know how many witnesses Christopher's side called, but it had to be at least twenty plus. They called old bosses, neighbors, their whole family and even one of the counselors at my high school. I had never met this counselor, but she knew of my family and knew both of my brothers, and that somehow made her an expert on me. I wondered what these people must be thinking. Did they realize their testimony would have an impact on if I would get to raise my son or not? That makes what they said extremely important, but I am not sure they thought of it that way.

I would think that the high school counselor would have reached out to me while I was in high school after the plane crash, yet I never knew her nor heard of her. I graduated early from high school with honors, yet she felt she could criticize me for moving away from everything I knew. A lot of people do that; the early pioneers certainly did!

Even though I wasn't close to my brother I warned him that they were trying to serve him to force him to testify. I knew they would make a big deal out of the fact that he was a homosexual and he had AIDS. I couldn't afford anything else damning about my case as I had already done enough to hurt my cause. I asked him to stay low as I didn't want him involved; for once he did as I asked.

I don't know how many days I was on the stand, but I told the truth the entire time, even about the affair. I explained the sexual and mental abuse which held me captive to the relationship and which ultimately resulted in us getting married. I talked about how the emotional and sexual abuse escalated during the marriage. I had to explain in detail about specific sexual events that negatively impacted me.

One example was allowing my husband to pee on me while I lay in the bathtub. My attorney called this "golden rain," all I knew was that it was humiliating and controlling, but when I protested he would tell me I must be gay like my brother if I didn't like it. Other times he would indicate he could find a hooker if I didn't want to perform for him. I didn't know what else to do but to follow his directions as I had no one to compare my circumstances with.

I was totally sexually naïve. However, the affair provided me with the awareness that this behavior was not typical at all; it was beastly and I was allowing it out of ignorance. That was when I realized I wanted out and wanted my son raised differently, away from his father. The details of my sharing my intimate life were humiliating, embarrassing, and forever life-changing. I would never allow someone to control me again. I would never allow myself to be considered an object nor would I ever be a victim of a man again.

I admitted that I not only worked and went to night school, but did most all the house chores as well; all the while Christopher sat in front of the TV in his underwear drinking beer. His attorney countered when Christopher was on the stand by showing a few examples of when he did indeed help out around the house in the five years we were married. He did this in an attempt to prove I was lying.

First Christopher explained he brought the ladder in to change a stairwell light bulb that had burned out. Next he referenced that the Christmas I was pregnant, he had gotten the Christmas ornaments down out of the attic for me. He wanted to also inform the jury that there was the situation with the John Deere riding lawnmower. We were the only one of our neighbors with a riding lawn mower. He used this to counter my testimony that I was mowing the yard the Saturday before Nick was born in August in 98% humidity. He agreed that I was mowing the yard, but come on, I was not using a push mower, I was using a riding mower. That sums up our marriage. It was a joke.

Christopher's parents had tape recorded phone calls I had with them. They felt the phone calls were indicative of my money-driven focus and my sudden desire for freedom as well as my lack of interest in being a good parent. I had called begging for their intervention, explaining that we were mortgaging our child's future with all the attorney bills. Couldn't we come up with a settlement and visitation schedule? I don't have a family; why would I not want my son to have a family?

I offered to pay for Christopher to go back to college and get a degree as he had dropped out of college after his third semester, I think it was. They said it was all between Christopher and me, and they couldn't help. The phone calls were played last for the jury to hear. I cried, as in my mind I could feel where my heart was—focused on Nick and not revenge nor hatefulness. My attorney was disgusted with me as he warned me not to call any of them. Court adjourned for the last time as we headed out for lunch.

Now my son's fate was in the jury's hands. I have never been so scared. My whole body was trembling, and I felt I was going to pass out.

Every day my attorney and I would leave the courthouse and walk a block to a local deli for a sandwich. This day was no exception. As we walked to lunch each day, my head hung down as I felt the weight of the world. This final day was no exception. On the way back to the courthouse, we crossed the street where we did every day, except this time someone had written a message in chalk that was facing me on the side walk "Smile, God Loves You!" I cried as I knew that message was for me.

Once again, even though I hadn't been going to church, I still prayed. God had not forgotten me in the least. He was right beside me during all the pain and hurt. I knew it was going to be alright. "Thank you, Lord, oh thank you!" My heart skipped a beat. I was still shaking, but a calmness fell over me as if I wasn't alone anymore.

The jury walked in and I began to cry as there was so much tension in the air. The verdict was read, "The plaintiff (me) gets full custody of the minor child." It was a unanimous vote. I got him! I couldn't breathe. I slid down in my chair and wept, and then somehow I got the energy to get up and shake every juror's hand and thank them on their way out. I wanted them to know I would always cherish the opportunity they gave me to raise my son. God had blessed me again; first with the birth of my baby, then with being awarded full custody of him. "Thank you, Lord, for loving me and loving my son!"

My attorney told me this wasn't over yet as the judge

still had to decide the visitation schedules as well as how to assign the marriage estate debts. At that point I didn't care; I just wanted to see my son. I left the courthouse and went straight to pick up Nick. He felt so good in my arms. I swore at that moment I would dedicate my life to raising him the best I could and most, important of all, to show him unconditional love.

CHAPTER 17
The Next Wave Hit

"Even if you cannot always see that silver lining on your clouds, God can, for He is the very source of the light you seek. He does love you, and He knows your fears. He hears your prayers. He is your Heavenly Father, and surely He matches with His own the tears His children shed."

Jeffrey R. Holland

Christopher filed a motion to claim half of my dad's farm. This farm was something personal to me. As a child growing up, we spent every weekend there. My dad bought the farm from my grandfather when I was born. There is no way Christopher could claim half of my farm. It was like someone had sucked all the air out of my lungs. This was the first time I actually thought I could be capable of killing someone. I hated him. I hated how he took my innocence. I hated how he used me to get at my money. I hated how he emotionally and sexually tortured me. I hated that he had hurt my son, and now he wants my dad's most prized possession, his farm.

I actually thought about paying someone to break his knee caps, but it was a fleeting thought. I didn't know how to hurt someone or kill someone. I didn't even want to feel the hatred that I felt toward him, but I did. I cried and I prayed. How much more could I be expected to endure? I felt like a wild animal that had been caged and was pacing, waiting for my next move, waiting to attack as I had been provoked over and over again.

There were several months of arguing, filing motions, crying, praying, hating, etc. All of this is poison to the soul. Then every six weeks, I would have to take my son back to that horrible place with people with no conscience. I hated leaving him in Houston. When I would get him back, he wasn't potty-trained anymore. He would pick up sticks and hit me and say, "I hate mommy. Kill mommy!" He would have fits of anger and screaming. He would hit me and kick me.

I continued to remember my promise, "unconditional love always." I would hold him until he would calm down. He would kick and bite me. I was bloody and bruised more times than I can count. I would work to get him potty-trained again. He would finally get back into a normal pattern and rhythm, then six weeks was up and it time for a visit back to Houston. It was torture seeing my son go through this.

Jeremiah 29:11, *"For I know the plans I have for you,"* declares the Lord, *"plans to prosper and not to harm you, plans to give you hope and a future."* Hope and a future; for me it all seemed pretty dismal at this point in my life. I felt God had abandoned me. I felt myself sinking into the abyss and not knowing where to turn to get my life back on track.

Finally the divorce was settled. I had to pay for my son's attorney fees, half of Christopher's attorney fees, and my attorney fees, which were over $120,000. I had to pay off our combined debt and out of the $50,000 I had invested in our home for our son's college tuition, I got about $4,000 back. I was in debt to my eyeballs, but I was through and I still had ownership of my father's farm. I had survived.

I felt I could rebuild in time as long as I had my son. I did not know what plans God had for my future, but I knew that I was now a survivor. I could hold my son close to my heart and feel his love in return. That was the greatest and most inspiring feeling, and that kept me pushing forward.

CHAPTER 18

Another Door Closes

"... it isn't just our sins Christ suffered and died for, but also our sorrows, our disappointments, heartaches, and embarrassment. All of it that's why he says even as he is being crucified, 'Father, forgive them, they know not what they are doing.'"

Glenn Beck

Reflecting back on my relationship with my brother, I realized he was always a difficult person to be around. Even growing up, we didn't get along. At the time, I didn't know what it was; I just knew he was different. After the accident I thought at first he was having problems trying to be the parent while trying to adapt to his loss of family as well, then he wanted all the family pictures taken down and there couldn't be any mention of the family. Again, I assumed this was his way of coping with the tragedy.

Arguments between us intensified. He began drinking alcohol daily and being drunk most of the time, and this was when he became his meanest. I wasn't aware that he was doing drugs at the same time, which probably accounted for most of the mood swings. He would say hateful things about my father or mother, which in turn forced me to stand up for them, then a heated argument would ensue. One time I got so mad I threw a frying pan at his head and luckily missed him. My home life with him was dysfunctional to say the least.

I kept thinking, as time went on, things would change between us, but they only got worse. In addition to the arguing, there were legal issues between us regarding the estates; then, he told me he was homosexual. At first I didn't believe him. I thought he was trying to hurt me again but sure enough, he was gay. That news took quite some time for me to absorb and process as I didn't understand, yet he was still my brother, so I was conflicted about what to think or feel.

At one point we went about nine years without talking unless it was through an attorney or in court. It was painful as I longed for family and he was all I had. I would send him birthday cards and Christmas cards but never heard from him. He didn't even know when his nephew was born as I didn't want him around spoiling the moment for me.

A few months before I filed for divorce (1986), he called. He wanted me to know he had AIDS and was dying. Over the course of several years, he had told so many lies, I naturally didn't believe him. It was a difficult phone call, but eventually he convinced me to meet him at a bar. I assumed he had run out of money and was coming to me for help.

―― *Living Through The Pain* ――

As soon as he walked in, I wanted to pass out. My brother was about six foot one and was truly a handsome man. He missed his calling to be a model, as I thought he had the look for it. Now here he was in front of me with lesions on his face, and his body was so swollen. I knew at that moment he was telling the truth. I was overwhelmed with guilt for not believing him and sadness as I didn't know what to do. We had wasted so much time between us.

AIDS was a fairly new disease, and most people thought they could contract AIDS just by being touched by someone with AIDS. Over time, research revealed that wasn't the case, but at this point in time, there was a public panic about this disease.

I was lost and didn't know how to interact with him as I was scared. He was my brother, and I longed for a relationship with him. His eyes told me he knew I was afraid and uncomfortable. We talked, and I could feel his pain and fear. He wanted to meet his nephew. I told him that I knew Christopher would never agree to that. The conversation quickly became tense. I assumed he was tired of being rejected by people. Before he left, he had to ensure he left me with plenty to think about.

First, he wanted me to know that he had carried a secret with him for many years. My mother had confided in him that she had had an affair with a tennis coach and had conceived him and me by this man. I suppose this was his way of ultimately trying to ruin any memories I had of my mom. At first I was shocked and in disbelief, but I yearned for family so bad that I became excited. I told him this was great news as I had a family out there somewhere and that we must find them! I am sure this startled him as he thought I would crumble by hearing the news, yet instead I was elated.

After he gave me a few minutes to process this, he had one more surprise for me. He told me that he hated our parents so bad that he had them moved from the cemetery to a place where no one would ever see them again. My heart froze as I intently looked into his eyes. How could he be so cruel? I demanded to know why he did this and where they were. He simply smiled and left.

My heart was racing, and I felt my world crumbling around me again. I drove home and had Christopher drive me to the cemetery. Certainly this was a lie as well. My brain was a whirlwind of emotions—I had another family, my brother is sick and dying, and my parents have been stolen from me. Sure enough, when we arrived at the cemetery, the grave marker had been removed. I didn't wait for Christopher; I ran all the way to the cemetery office, but it was Saturday and they were closed. I fell to the ground crying. He stole my parents! Why would he be so cruel? I felt so sick and empty on the inside. I was dazed and confused, and I suppose I was also in shock. My breathing was shallow, and I felt faint as I lay outside the cemetery office door.

The weekend was pure hell for me. The only thing I could focus on was my parents being taken. When Monday morning came, I was at the cemetery office waiting for them to open. I was in a total state of panic. They looked up the records and indicated that my parents hadn't been moved. My brother had noticed that the cemetery mower had chipped off a piece of the bronze grave marker and he requested it to be replaced.

The cemetery staff had removed the marker to fix it and it would be about six weeks before the marker was replaced. Can you imagine the suffering I endured that entire weekend all for nothing? Fast forward to my divorce trial; Christopher used this incident to make it sound like we went to the cemetery for a visit and the grave marker was gone so, based on my erratic behavior and mental state at the time, I jumped to the conclusion that my parents had been stolen. He never explained the real story to the jury. Naturally, to the jury, it must have looked like I was crazy.

I called my brother and he laughed. He said he knew he could so easily flip my switch because I was a crazy person when it came to them. He then went on to tell me that the story of my mom's affair was a lie. He thought it would tarnish her image with me, but instead I seemed excited to have a family somewhere out there instead of appreciating the fact that I had him. I couldn't speak; I could only hang up on him. How was I supposed to love someone so hateful? How was I supposed to respond to such cruelty? My brain couldn't handle such extreme cruelty. I began to feel I was going crazy. I felt I couldn't bear much more.

Nevertheless, as my divorce moved forward, I allowed Kerry periodic visits with my son, but I remained extremely cautious. Any dishes Kerry used, I threw away. I would let Kerry play with him, but Kerry wasn't allowed to hold or touch him. He respected my directives. He genuinely seemed to love his nephew as he was the future of our family.

With the money Kerry had, he had the means to purchase all different kinds of drugs to help him fight the disease but in time, the disease won out. He had survived about five years, which was a long time back in the late eighties. He was scared to die and scared of the pain he would have to endure. I made myself available to be there for him. He called me several times each night and would cry on the phone and ask, "Why? Why did this have to happen to me?" He was jealous that I had a child and eventually would be able to have a future with someone I loved. I listened to him and tried to be as supportive as I could, but it was taking a toll on me.

I traveled back to Houston as much as I could to spend time with him. He was scheduled to visit me at Christmas in 1989. I had even turned down a lucrative job offer as they wanted me to start the first of December and I said I couldn't start until January due to my brother's visit. They withdrew the offer. I don't know if it was because I wanted to delay my start date or the fact that I had a brother with AIDS. People were scared of this disease.

I had taken my son to the airport early Christmas Eve for his flight to Houston to visit his dad and grandparents and was waiting for Kerry to come out on Christmas Day and spend a week with me. I didn't think about the fact that we hadn't spoken in a few days. When I got home from taking Nick to the airport, the phone rang. It was Kerry's doctor. He told me Kerry was in the hospital and declining rapidly. He didn't have much hope that he would even make it through the night.

I had promised my brother that I would be there for him and, damn it, I had to keep that promise. I prayed for God's help. I called and got a flight out at midnight and made it to Houston by eight the next morning. Even with all the problems between me and my ex-in-laws, I called them and asked if they could pick me up and get me to the hospital. They graciously said yes. That was an awfully long flight. I cried all the way home and didn't sleep a wink on the plane.

When I arrived in Houston, my ex-in-laws told me they had stopped by the hospital on the way to the airport and that Kerry was still alive. They rushed me to the hospital and not a word was said in the car. I simply couldn't talk to anyone.

When we arrived at his hospital room, my ex-father-in-law advised that I should first casually walk by the door, look in and keep walking. It would help me process what he looked like so I could be prepared and not fall apart when I walked in. He was right. When I saw Kerry, I felt like I had been punched in the gut. How was I going to overcome my fear and walk in and not fall apart? I took some deep breaths and quickly asked God for strength to endure what I had to face.

I quietly walked into his room and held his cold, boney hand. He already looked dead. His lips were splitting open due to lack of moisture, and he had a horrible smell. I got a sponge from the nurse and began wiping his mouth slowly to clean up his lips and provide him moisture, then I used a straw and dropped some little squirts of water into his mouth.

He was on oxygen and had many IVs and electrical devices hooked to him. There was a body, but really just bones and skin lying in a bed. I have never felt such compassion for someone. Here is my brother in so much pain and I couldn't help him. I had promised to take him home. After consulting with the doctor, I was told he was on lethal doses of morphine and should already be dead, but he was fighting it.

I called one of his friends to pick up some familiar items from his home, like a quilt, some pictures, a pillow, and stuffed animals, so maybe he would feel like he was home. I knew in my heart I was breaking my promise, but I didn't know what else to do. I stayed with him except for one time when I went to the chapel to pray. I prayed God would forgive him of his sins and take him home as he had suffered enough. I literally begged God to take him home.

I have to admit I always felt there was a story behind my brother that I didn't know. He never broke down after the accident, and he actually enjoyed the attention by the reporters. He never showed any indication that he ever missed our family. Actually, a few months earlier he told me he knew what had happened. At the time of the accident, Kerry was taking flying lessons himself, so he was familiar with planes and how they worked. If you recall, I never remembered where Kerry slept the night before the accident or even if he did.

He told me that someone had loosened the rudder bolt on the plane and, after the plane was in flight, a few too many moves of the rudder and the bolt would come off and Ronnie would lose control of the plane. He said it

Living Through The Pain

so matter of fact that again, I never knew when to believe him or when not to. All I knew was as time went on; he had a deep hatred for my father and even deeper jealousy of Ronnie. I wanted to ask if he caused the plane to crash or if he knew of someone who did. Unfortunately, the whole time I was with him at the hospital, he couldn't talk; only his eyes could follow me. I wanted to ask him, but I couldn't. He was on his death bed, and all I felt was pity for him and sadness for what we both had lost.

Later I would learn about a new story regarding the plane crash based upon information I learned from exploring his counseling session notes.

Kerry's counseling session January 9, 1989: "Kerry reported that yesterday he was contacted at home by someone conducting an investigation into circumstances surrounding the plane crash that killed his family—said that some evidence had turned up suggesting that there had been foul play (tampering with rudder of plane)—business associate of father's under suspicion—Kerry reports that he had suspected this all along—Kerry reports that he furnished information that he knew about and made it clear to investigator that Cathy knew nothing about this and was not, under any circumstances, to be contacted about this—also wanted my assurance that I would never discuss with Cathy—Kerry expressed that Cathy had suspected foul play and had struggled with putting this out of her mind, feared that if this were opened up for her that she might lose control, might even attempt to murder father's business associate." This was the first I had learned of this scenario.

Early in the morning on December 27th, I stood over him and rubbed his hair. I told him I knew he was afraid to die, but he didn't need to be. I knew he was afraid to see Daddy, but the way I looked at it, Daddy was proud of him as he had endured so much pain. Yes, he made bad decisions, but his life wasn't easy; and there is God; well, God forgives us if just ask Him to. So I asked him to repent in his heart to God. If he asked with a truthful heart to be forgiven, God would forgive and welcome him home, and he would be released from this pain. I truly believed that. He turned his head toward me and tears rolled out of his eyes. I told him I loved him, then I held his hand.

Finally my body was giving in to the lack of sleep. I told him I was going to lie on the couch beside him, and he only needed to make a rattle of the bed rail and I would be up if he needed me. I had just laid down when I heard a noise that sounded like a gasp. I waited for second as I wasn't sure what I had heard; then I heard it again. I jumped up and ran to his side, but he was gone. I pulled off the oxygen mask to see if he was breathing and he wasn't. I stood there quietly crying in the dark and in shock. My brother was gone, and I was totally alone in the world with no family. He was barely 34 and I had just turned 30. Life was changing for me, and once again I was still that lonely figure crying in the dark.

I learned many years after his death that my intuition about his fear was correct. Reading Kerry's counseling session notes confirmed that he indeed was afraid of meeting my father on the other side of death.

Kerry's counseling session September 24, 1986: ". . .

still fears sometimes meeting them (parents) after death, talked about concept of death—possibility of another dimension and that even if they are there, parents don't have power, also has ideas about reincarnation and expressed thought that 'maybe they're back already.'"

October 29, 1986 session stated, ". . . focused on his concerns about death and talked more about possibilities of afterlife—still raises fears about encountering parents."

CHAPTER 19
Final Closure

"Teach us how short our lives really are so that we may be wise."

Psalms 90:12

After Kerry died I had so many unanswered questions. He had lied to me so much over the years I didn't know what to believe anymore. I had to jump through numerous legal hurdles, but I was finally successful in obtaining his records from the counseling center he attended. The records covered the periods of March 1984 through his last session in November 1989, one month before he died.

The agreement that was reached with Kerry's attorney was that I could only obtain these records if they were sent to a counselor of my choice in California. My brother's counselor felt the records contained enough sensitive information that I shouldn't be reading it alone and without the support of a professional counselor to assist me in processing the information. I agreed to those terms.

Living Through The Pain

It was several years before I felt I was emotionally strong enough to go through the records. Each session, I would read a few pages out loud to my therapist, and then she would assist me in processing the material and putting it into the proper perspective. This was an extremely difficult time for me. When Kerry passed away, I hit a wall. We didn't get along, but at least I knew he was there. His death forced me into therapy, which also forced me to deal with the accident and the failure of my marriage. In the long run, this was actually what I needed, but it was painful.

I remember about a year and half into counseling I wanted to quit; literally quit life and commit suicide. I felt I couldn't take any more pain. I had, in my mind, slowly built a brick wall around my feelings regarding the accident, the way my brother had treated me, and the fact that my marriage had failed. To deal with Kerry's death, I had to tear the wall down brick by brick and deal with all of it. When I felt I had torn the wall down halfway, enough for me to climb over, I shut down out of fear. My therapist pushed me forward and said, "It is now or never. You have come so far. If you don't cross over the wall now and deal with your feelings, you will never be able to do so."

Luckily, I pushed forward. I had to, as I had a son who was counting on his mom to be there for him, and emotionally I needed to get my act together. Kerry's records were painful to read. The first page stated his reason for requesting services. He wrote, "Dissatisfied with life . . . financial difficulties stemming from effort to maintain facade of success and affluence . . . Terrified of loneliness. . . . Abusing alcohol periodically. . . I have no income, too many debts, and I'm scared! I want a relationship, but I can't seem to have one." That, in and of itself, breaks my heart. We both needed each other, but we couldn't find a way to connect.

Then I got to the delusional part of my brother's counseling notes: ". . . talked about missing his brother, Terry, who is classified as MIA in Vietnam for seventeen years—has had arguments with his sister over this; sister insists that Terry is dead, Kerry is not willing to accept this as final. (Note, we didn't have a brother named Terry) . . . Kerry believes that the plane crash that killed mother, father, brother, and sister-in-law was intentional—Kerry's brother was piloting the plane, Kerry believes Ronnie may have deliberately crashed plane to kill parents. . . . Mother locked him outside her room and fired gun into wall, waited fifteen minutes, while Kerry cried outside her door before coming out. He talked about physical and sexual abuse, about my mother putting vodka in his baby bottle, and my dad breaking his wrist."Lies, all lies, yet it was hard for me to read, much less understand why he said these things."

It took a long time to realize that my brother said these things because he believed them. He was sick, both mentally and physically. He was taking too many medications and going to different doctors who didn't know what the other doctors were prescribing him. In those days, it was difficult to track prescriptions. He was on high doses of Valium (from different doctors) while at the same time, one of his doctors was giving him antidepressant medicines and Brompton's mixture (morphine, cocaine, and several other narcotics, according to the therapy notes). He was also taking AZT for the AIDs and drinking and smoking heavily. All of this had to impair his ability to think rationally, much less truthfully.

I wish I had been capable of better understanding my brother, his pain, and his thoughts so I could have helped him cope. I always saw him as evil and wanting to deliberately hurt me, so I tried to stay away from him as much as possible. When we were together, we always fought, and the fights were verbally brutal.

I fortunately found a wonderful therapist who worked with me for years sorting through my past, my pain, my heartaches and my fears to finally find resolution and peace. In the end I came to terms with my past, or so I thought. However, I had rebuilt the brick wall around my emotions, memories, and pain, so I could remain strong. I don't know how others deal with their trauma, but this is how I deal with trauma so I can remain sane and enjoy my life.

I learned through one of my counseling books about self-reconciliation. "Perhaps one of the greatest gifts you can offer yourself is self-reconciliation. Isn't it time you acknowledge your past and understand that it has led you to this present moment? As you look back into your past, use the wisdom of hindsight to understand how your actions were sometimes driven by a lack of awareness and fear. This awareness will help you develop more compassion or a better understanding of how you got to be where are now." *A Mindful-Based Stress Reduction Workbook* by Bob Stahl, PH.D. and Elisha Goldstein, PH.D.

Kerry's untimely death propelled me to stop and look back over my past. I had to reconcile my pain and trauma to move forward, and I don't know if I would have ever done that without Kerry's death. When watching a loved one die, especially in a painful way, you change. It changes everything about a person and how you look at the world and at others. His death had a profound impact on me. I was lost in the world and simply keeping it all together for the sake of my son, but I was panic-stricken on the inside. I lived in fear, fear of losing my son, fear of dying before he grew up, fear of losing my job and not being able to support and raise my son.

By not embracing the fear, I couldn't fully embrace God and the love he had for me. Kerry's sad life and torturous death changed me for the better. I got the help I needed and faced down my demons. I owe my current life and my current relationship with God to Kerry. I pray he asked for God's forgiveness before he died as I certainly want to hug him when I die and meet him in heaven.

CHAPTER 20
A Door Opens and Quickly Closes

"When everything seems to be going against you, remember that the airplane takes off against the wind, not with it."

Henry Ford

Right before Kerry passed away I met a young man named Steve. I certainly wasn't looking to meet anyone, as Carl had broken my heart. Carl and I had finally broken up; not much of a surprise that I caught him cheating on me. With Carl out of my life, I had sworn off men. I had started a new job working for the State of California. I proudly displayed a picture of my son on my desk as he was so cute. Everyone who stopped by my desk kept mentioning that I needed to meet this guy named Steve as they felt my son looked just like him. Again, there was no interest on my part, but finally Steve stopped by to introduce himself. He was a tall, good looking man, but I didn't see the resemblance with my son at all. I had hoped now, people would just let it go.

Email was relatively new in the office and I was not familiar with it. That afternoon I got a message in my inbox from Steve. It was a nice simple email so I felt I had a pal. Little did I know that he would begin emailing me more and more every day, just light-hearted messages and joking around with me. It was fun to have a friend, so I always responded. I didn't feel any of the messages were inappropriate nor did I think either of us was flirting with the other. Finally Steve asked me to lunch. I declined, as I didn't want to go to lunch with him, but he kept insisting. I finally agreed.

We walked to lunch and had a nice conversation. He mentioned his kids and that he was married, but unhappily married. I sympathized with him as I had been there before, but I didn't encourage him one way or the other. After lunch I got more emails. The emails were now a daily ritual. Still being naïve, I thought of him as my pal.

One day after work the Assembly was holding a picnic at the Capital Park for staff. We both worked for the Assembly. He asked if I was going to attend and I told him no. He suggested I should go so he could introduce me to people. I finally agreed. When I got to the park, he took my backpack from me and said he would take it to his office so I didn't have to keep up with it. I thought that was a gentlemanly offer from him.

I stayed for about an hour and a half and decided I needed to get my backpack and head home. He walked me back to his office to get my backpack and that is when he leaned over and kissed me. I was stunned. I just stood there looking at him. I told him I didn't want to get involved with a married man. Carl and I had broken up and, when we started going out, he was married and I hated it. I wasn't going down that path again. He said he understood, then walked me to my car and kissed me again. I have never been smart with men. I just shook it off and went home.

Unfortunately, that night began the beginning of our relationship. He convinced me he was unhappy and had been for years and that he was getting a divorce. Obviously, I was just a damned fool who hadn't learned anything about romance, relationships, and men, and obviously I hadn't had enough of a broken heart. I fell for him hook, line, and sinker. We had a five year off and on again relationship that resulted in him getting divorced and us getting married and eventually us getting divorced. Our marriage lasted a total of fourteen months.

Everything I believed about him was a lie. Looking back, it seems to me that I was desperate once again to be loved by someone, anyone. He was conveniently there to help console me with the loss of my brother. He made me feel special, like I could conquer the world. I felt absolutely beautiful in his eyes, and I think he really believed he loved me, but he could never get over the guilt of divorcing his wife and only being with his kids part-time.

I broke off the marriage. When I met him, he drank heavily and went out to the bars all the time. He indicated to me that he did this because he was so unhappy at home. I thought when we got married, he had changed, but the guilt turned him back to the bottle and his old ways. One night my son asked me, "Why does Steve always come home smelling like alcohol?" That was it for me. I had my wake up call. My decision to marry Steve was negatively impacting Nick, so I filed for divorce. The marriage sadly ended.

I had hoped Steve would try and fight for our marriage, but he simply gave up. I, too, gave up on my dream of marriage and men. I think we both realized we had made an awful mistake and had hurt his former wife, his two children, my son, and ourselves in the process. Why was life so difficult and hard to get right? I figured that type of life wasn't in the cards for me and I would never put my son in a situation where he had a bad role model ever again. He had known Carl and hated him, and now here was Steve, whom he loved, yet was exhibiting poor choices in front of my son. I felt like I was a failure to my son.

It is sad to think I spent five years in a relationship that once again ended. There isn't much to tell about that part of my life as it is more of a blur to me as I think I was numb most of the time. I was still working on healing from my past traumas, and now I had one more loss in my life. My relationship with Steve should have never happened, but the failure of the marriage coupled with the passing of my brother forced me deeper into therapy for help as I was severely depressed.

I wondered if I would ever have a happy life or were there more wrong paths (choices) that I would be taking in the future? I so wanted a happy life, to be a good mom and to not feel like a failure. If I would have regularly read my Bible, the following passage would have been of immense healing for me: *"Don't be wishing you were someplace else or with someone else. Where you are right now is God's place for you. Live and obey and love and believe right there. God, not your marital status, defines your life." 1 Corinthians 7:17*

CHAPTER 21

God's Blessing

"Some blessings come soon, some come late, and some don't come until heaven; but for those who embrace the gospel of Jesus Christ, they come."

Created for Greater Things, Jeffrey R. Holland

While returning from visiting my brother in November 1989, I had to change planes in Denver. In Denver I requested a seat change to a window seat as I feel more comfortable when I can see out the window. It helps me remain calm while flying. The flight fortunately wasn't full so I was moved up toward the front of the plane and got a window seat.

Another lady was visiting her family in Colorado and she, too, requested a change of seats placing her more toward the front of the plane. She was given the aisle seat for the row I was on and the middle seat was vacant for the flight.

I was having some serious emotional issues trying to

hold back my tears. It was my father's birthday, I was flying and leaving behind my brother, whom I knew would probably die within a few months. I just wanted to keep to myself and process my thoughts until the plane landed in Sacramento. The lady in the aisle seat had other ideas. Her name was Holly and she was a talker. No matter how much I tried to ignore her, it simply wasn't possible. By the time we landed in Sacramento, she knew most of my life story and we had become friends.

Little did I know that my friendship with her would ultimately turn into a sisterhood between us, and she would have a significant impact on my life. Holly was always a supportive, loving person. She helped me through the pain of losing my brother and helped with the ups and downs of my relationship with Steve and our marriage and divorce. She was that friend in the darkness of the night when I was alone who I could call for a comforting voice and encouraging words.

She truly believed in me, was proud of me and loved me in spite of my faults and prior failures. She prayed daily for me. She was by all measures my sister, my friend.

In the fall of 1997 (late October), she called me at work to see how I was doing. I was in a depressed mood that day and shared with her that I felt God wanted me to be a single mom and eventually a single grandmother. I felt for certain my opportunities to ever find the "right" guy wasn't in the cards for me, and I was trying to come to terms with that as I felt I had so much love: I honestly wanted to share my life with someone, but I wasn't hopeful that would ever happen. She indicated she had to go and hung up on me. I thought that was a weird reaction but I had work to get back to so I let it slide.

A short time later, Holly called me back. She said she had heard God's voice in her head saying, "Dusk, Dusk." She knew at that moment she needed to call Dusk and get us together. Okay, at this point, I thought she had lost it. Since she had been a friend for such a long time, I wondered why she had never introduced me to Dusk before. She explained that Dusk had been married for several years, but that his wife had died from some type of heart and lung disease. It had been three years since her death, and he was ready to get out and start dating again, but he didn't feel comfortable and wasn't sure how to proceed. That's when Holly indicated that I could help him get over the hump by going out with him. After hearing his story, the compassionate side of me came out and I agreed, but one date only. After all, what kind of guy has a name of Dusk?

Dusk called me that night and we talked a long time. He was so easy to talk to. I immediately felt comfortable with him. I was looking forward to our date on Saturday night, but only as a way of helping him, not as someone I would be dating. Saturday night came, and when the doorbell rang, I had an immediate knot in my stomach. I felt scared for some reason. Upon opening the door, I saw a nice looking man, and he was smiling.

We had both agreed upon a restaurant ahead of time, but when we got there, they had gone out of business. Okay, we were off to a rocky start already. Even with that bump, we both looked at each other and laughed. Soon, he found another restaurant. I had trouble eating my meal. The meal was great but we were too busy talking and enjoying each other's company. We had so much in common. We talked about life's tragedies, family, values, and God. We were comfortable talking about God on our first date; now that was impressive.

When he brought me back home, he told me goodnight and gave me a quick hug, but no kiss. I definitely wasn't used to this. I wasn't sure if he liked me or not. Stop it, I thought, this wasn't a date, but I kept thinking about him.

The next morning after church he called to see if he could take a ride out to see me. Of course I said yes. We spent several hours just talking and getting to know one another. Again when he left, he briefly hugged me, but no kiss.

The following day when I got home from work, one of the neighbors came over with some flowers that had been delivered. I opened the card and it read, "Just because, Dusk." I was shocked; what did this mean? When I called to thank him he said I had been through so much that he felt it had been a long time since someone had done something nice for me so he wanted to send me some beautiful flowers just because. That took my breath away. No man had ever been so sweet before.

Every night we talked on the phone for a couple of hours and began to get to know one another. When he asked about getting together over the weekend, I couldn't believe it, but I said I couldn't see him until after Christmas. I went on to explain that our neighborhood is crazy about Christmas. We put up hundreds of lights on each house and we draw Disney characters on plywood, cut them out, paint them, and place them in our yards. This is our gift to those who come into our neighborhood over the holidays as well as to each other.

He hadn't decorated for Christmas the last three years due to the loss of his wife. He was excited to hear what our project was and asked if he could help. Well, we did need someone to help us pick up the plywood and he did have a truck. We didn't have a power saw to cut the characters out, so okay, we could use his help, but he had to understand this was a long project taking numerous hours, so no dating until after Christmas. He was sold.

He was so much help to Nick and me as we would have never been able to pull off our part of the project without his help. Nick had decided that year that he wanted to do a holiday room in our third car garage. He envisioned a snowman theme with black lights lighting up his fake snow. I had no idea what he wanted to do, but thankfully Dusk offered to help him. Dusk didn't try to do it for him, but rather taught him how to use the skill saw, electric drill, etc. The snow room turned out beautifully.

On December 7th, we had the neighborhood tree lighting ceremony which was in our side yard. The neighborhood was all lit up and it finally felt like Christmas. That night I asked Dusk to be there to sit outside with us as the cars drove by and the people walked the neighborhood. As people stopped by and thanked us for the beautiful display, I caught a glimmer of a tear rolling down Dusk's face. I asked if he was okay and he said yes. It had been a long time since he had experienced the

Living Through The Pain

holiday spirit, and this was awesome.

The next night, it was cold outside. The Christmas lights were twinkling. The neighbor across the street had a fog machine going, and people were singing Christmas carols. We strolled the neighborhood hand-in-hand and we began to fall in love.

By Valentine's Day we were engaged, and on June 13th, we got married. A few days before the wedding, I had a panic attack. At around 2:30 in the morning I ran into Nick's room crying. I turned his light on and woke him up. I told him I was calling off the wedding as he had been through enough with me, and until he graduated from high school, it was going to be just me and him as he was the "man of the house."

He sat up in bed, shook his head, and wisely told me, "Mom, if you don't marry Dusk, it will be the biggest mistake you have ever made. Now go back to bed." I kissed him, tucked him back in bed, turned off his light and slowly walked back to my room. I wondered how my son got so smart.

June 13, 1998, we did indeed get married. I have never regretted marrying Dusk as it definitely was the best thing I ever did outside of having my son. After the wedding, Dusk and I rushed back to our side of town to watch "our" son play in one of his Little League Baseball games. How many men would start their honeymoon at a Little League game?

In my marriage to Dusk, he has always placed our son as the top priority. Due to baseball practices and games, track practices and meets, and homework every night, there were many late dinners or fast food dinners, no time on the weekends, and little couple time. Dusk has been a great father. He loves my son as his own child. God blessed me with an honest, hardworking, Godly man to be the head of our household, and I thank God for that blessing every night before I close my eyes.

CHAPTER 22

Trusting God

*"We know the love God has for us,
and we trust that love."*

1 Christopher 4:16

When Dusk and I got married, I still had many demons to deal with. I had no self-confidence and was suffering from fear of not being loved. I was still riddled with guilt and shame and felt a dark cloud hovering over my every move. My prior three relationships had all been failures. I was so desperate to find love and to be loved that I sought out love with the wrong type of men. As a result, each relationship failed.

I knew I loved Dusk, but I doubted myself. I continually asked Dusk when he was going to leave me. His answer was always the same, "I am not going anywhere. I love you." I had such doubts regarding love that I couldn't accept his answer as being honest. Most men would have fled with my continual verbal doubts about our relationship, but not Dusk. He is a man after God's own heart. He stood his ground and remained faithful to me and our marriage. He could see inside me, what I couldn't see in myself. I had a kind, loving heart, and I loved the Lord, yet I was consumed with shame, guilt, and self-punishment.

As the years went by, our relationship grew and became stronger, and slowly my self-doubt started diminishing. I needed to see that he loved me and he wasn't going to leave. He eventually proved his love to me. The more time went by, the more confident I became and the more I was able to open my heart to really love again. God was working on my heart, softening it and slowly expelling the fear, the shame, and the guilt that I had carried for decades. From day one, Dusk had been secure in himself and his love of us. In time, the three of us merged into a strong family.

As the years went by, my confidence grew and I began to realize that Dusk loved me for me. He wasn't going to leave me or hurt me. Love is supposed to be kind, gentle, and supportive, not judgmental or harsh or accusatory. For once I had the love I had yearned so long for. I felt loved and safe for the first time since I was sixteen. It had been a tough and bumpy road to get to this point in my life. However, in the back of my mind was still the thought, when is the next shoe going to fall? Satan had been embedded in my soul for so long controlling my thoughts that I hadn't been successful in purging this remaining doubt. I always seemed a little restless as I just wasn't sure a happy ending was ever in the cards for me. I trusted God but I doubted myself and my worthiness to have love.

A few years into the marriage, Dusk started having

health problems. He could feel that something was wrong with his heart. We went from doctor to doctor and emergency room to emergency room, but nothing ever showed up. Here was this young, vibrant man who was aging before my eyes. It was difficult to see him with shortness of breath and little to no energy without any answers as to what was wrong.

Doctors began to treat us as if his symptoms were imaginary. We both were frustrated as his health was declining but no one was taking us seriously. Finally, in an effort to appease us, his doctor placed a heart monitor on him and asked him to lay in the patient room and when he felt he was having a heart problem, he was to click the red button which would record the event. The doctor told us we could stay in the room all day if we needed to. I could tell he felt we were wasting his time, but at least we had a shot of recording something.

After a few hours, Dusk felt the pain and had shortness of breath. He clicked the red button and the machine began to record his heart beats. We were elated that maybe we would finally get some answers. When the doctor came in, he looked at the recording and indicated that Dusk had mitral valve prolapse. He explained that in mitral valve prolapse, when the left ventricle contracts, one or both flaps of the mitral valve flops back into the left atrium. This prevents the valve from forming a tight seal. As a result, blood could leak from the ventricle back into the atrium. The backflow of blood is called regurgitation.

Many people who have mitral valve prolapse never experience any related symptoms or problems. When backflow does occur, shortness of breath, irregular heartbeats, and chest pain can occur. Finally, we had a diagnosis, and it wasn't as bad as we initially thought it might be. Dusk was placed on blood pressure medicine and told he would be just fine.

We accepted that diagnosis for about a year thinking in time things would get better and he would get use to the symptoms he was having. Instead, the symptoms seemed to get worse and his health appeared to still be declining. We again started seeing heart specialists and even pulmonary specialists, but nothing ever turned up from the various tests performed. By now Dusk seemed to be barely hanging in there, and I lived daily with the fear of losing him before we could find out what was actually wrong.

The cardiologist finally decided to administer a transesophageal echocardiogram (TEE). An endoscope would be run down his throat into his esophagus. At the end of the scope was a high-frequency ultrasound transducer which produced a graphic outline of the heart's movement. The doctor would be able to then check out his heart valves and heart chambers.

Over the course of a couple of months, the doctor performed two TEEs. All were unremarkable. Still no diagnosis, and Dusk's health was continuing to decline. Finally, out of sheer desperation, I insisted that the doctor perform another TEE, but during the afternoon. The two prior TEEs were all performed around 7:00 AM. Dusk always seemed to be at his worst in the afternoon, so I reasoned they should be able to see something if he worked the first half of the day, then the TEE was performed.

The doctor finally agreed.

After Dusk was taken back into the surgical room, his cardiologist told me he didn't think he would find anything different from the last two tests. I waited and prayed that God would guide the doctor in finding out what was wrong with my husband.

About fifteen minutes went by and the doctor came out. He was pale and looked distraught. He had a black and white picture in his hand. He said if he wouldn't have seen it himself, he wouldn't have believed it. He showed me the picture which reflected there was a tear in Dusk's mitral valve and, when he exerts himself, the blood spews out like a geyser. He indicated Dusk needed valve surgery sooner than later.

The doctor would have to take it before the medical group's surgical team for approval as Dusk was only 48 and typically surgeons do not like performing valve surgery before the patient is 60. Dusk would have a choice of a pig's valve (which would last about ten years) or a mechanical valve, but he would then have to take blood thinners for the rest of his life. In the meantime, he said I would have to watch him because if the hole tore, he could potentially bleed out before he could make it to the hospital.

I was crushed. I didn't know how to process this. What if the medical group didn't approve the surgery? We couldn't afford it, but without it, he could die. We felt vindicated that a complete diagnosis was finally made, but how could we be happy with the outcome? It took about thirty days before the medical group approved the surgery, then we had to wait to get approval for a cardio-surgeon, schedule an appointment and get in to see him. This took another two weeks. I felt I was aging overnight as I was constantly worried and could barely sleep. Dusk kept going to work and just trying to make it day by day.

Finally, in October 2003, he was scheduled for his surgery. We were told the surgery would run between six and seven hours. Dusk's family and many of my friends and co-workers were scheduled to come to the waiting room at the hospital and wait with me. The night before the surgery, Dusk and I sat on the couch and talked about the "what if." He was calm and not the least bit worried. He assured me that God had brought him this far, and whatever God chose to do would be fine with him. He was at peace with everything. I couldn't imagine he wasn't scared. He said God was in control; what did he have to be sacred of? I had such little faith. My old doubts and fears were creeping back in again. I felt I couldn't breathe. I was terrified of losing him, the only person who really loved me, besides Nick.

That night I quietly prayed to God for his assistance and his watching over the doctors and nurses. I tried to go to sleep, but I was too anxious; then my heart changed. I got up and knelt beside the bed, and with tears streaming down my face I prayed again to God. I thanked him for Dusk, a love that I didn't know I would ever find. I thanked him for blessing us with Dusk in our lives and then I acknowledged what Dusk had told me a long time ago about my parents, "God picked the most beautiful flowers in the garden for heaven and that is why he chose your parents."

I told God that Dusk, too, is a beautiful flower and I would understand. I now do understand, if he wants him, I will freely let him go in peace as I am grateful for the time God has lent him to me. With that I was finally able to release and peacefully go to sleep.

The next morning came and I was still at peace. I didn't want to lose Dusk, but God had been so wonderful in granting me the time I had with Dusk to know what "real love" was all about, how could I be selfish? I just keep thinking, "Let God's will be done and let God help me to be strong and accept that will."

The surgeon told me, after two hours into the surgery, the surgical nurse would come out and give me an update. Our group filled the waiting room. We read scripture, we prayed, and we sang hymns. The others in the waiting room joined us. They, too, had loved ones also having serious heart surgery. Our love of God gave them peace.

The waiting room was a wonderful place filled with love and God's grace. After two hours, the nurse came out to give me an update. She indicated he would be out of surgery in about twenty minutes. I didn't understand, as the surgery had barely started. She said everything went perfectly; the surgeon was able to repair the tear and place a titanium ring around the valve so it would hold its shape. He would be in the ICU as soon as they had a bed ready for him. I had to sit down. My husband was going to be fine. They didn't have to replace his valve.

What a miracle! I had turned my husband over to God, and He gave him back to me all fixed. God is so good. I had learned to unconditionally trust in whatever God's outcome was to be, and He blessed me beyond my dreams! The ICU wasn't prepared for him for several more hours so it took them more time to get an ICU bed ready for him than the surgery took.

When I think back to that day, there is no question but God was in the waiting room and heard our faithful prayers and songs to him. *"For I can do everything through Christ, who gives me strength." Philippians 4:13*. When the nurses allowed me into the ICU unit to see him, he was on an ice bed which kept his core body temperature low. There were numerous tubes coming out of his body and all sorts of electronic gadgets hooked up to him. His skin was grayish-blue.

It was so hard to see him like that as it didn't seem real. I grabbed onto his toes and wouldn't let go. I could feel him wiggle his toes for me, and I knew in my heart he was going to be fine. Later the next day he was moved out of the ICU and into his own room. From there he had to get up several times a day and slowly walk down the hall.

Trying to sit up to get out of bed was a struggle for him as his sternum ached from being split in two. He also had to endure tortuous muscle spasms in his back. The nurses indicated that this was a common problem as separating the rib cage and opening it for the surgery greatly impacts the back muscles. Dusk indicated that the muscle spasms were the most painful part of the whole episode. After five days I got to take him home, then after three weeks he returned to work and hasn't looked back.

Revisiting this time in our life brings me great comfort as I felt closer to God during that time than I ever have. I completely felt God was listening to my prayers and smiling down on me saying, "Child, do not fret. Your husband will be fine. I have plenty more for the both of you to do before I call either of you home." There is nothing like the fear of losing a spouse to remind you of all the blessings God has provided over the years as well as the opportunity to reflect on the love you have for your spouse.

As I am working on this book, we just celebrated fifteen years of blissful marriage. It hasn't been difficult at all. We have endured heart surgeries, serious illnesses, moving our son to college in Nebraska, then moving him back to California after he graduated, moving into a new home, losing jobs, and even severe financial problems, but never has our marriage been a chore to either of us.

It has been like we have known each other and been together forever. We complement each other and feel God provided us with our other half to make us whole. Dusk is supportive of me, my struggles from the past, my desires to be the best mom I can be, and my desire to know what God wants of me and our family so we can honor God. Through all my pain and trauma, God has enormously blessed me with Dusk and Nick in my life. I couldn't possibly ask for more.

CHAPTER 23

Finding Strength from God

"He gives strength to those who are tired and more power to those who are weak. The people who trust the Lord will become strong again. They will rise up as an eagle in the sky; they will run and not rest; they will walk and not become tired."

Isaiah 40:29, 31

In 2009, I was blessed in receiving a state job with a promotion to Deputy Director of Administrative Services. This job provided me an opportunity to utilize all my managerial experience in the following areas: Accounting, Budgets, Contracts, Procurement, Audits, Information Technology, Human Resources (HR) and Business Services. The people I worked with in this department were well educated and extremely passionate about the services the department provided to customers throughout the state.

I, too, brought a passionate commitment to the job and rejoiced as I was able to oversee streamlining efforts for all departmental policies and procedures. In a short period of time, I had accomplished some major changes which had been severely needed by the department over the last several years. The pride I was experiencing from this job, coupled with my happy home life, left me with a false sense of security as all was well with my life.

In mid-October of that year I was informed that my boss had accepted another state position with a different department and the Director and herself wanted to personally ask me to begin supervising one of her more challenging staff, Barbara. I agreed to take on this staff person knowing she had an unusual work schedule and sometimes she was difficult to get along with but I had no feeling of concern. After I accepted the request, I was informed that the individual I would now be supervising had been diagnosed with schizophrenia and bi-polar disorders. I still wasn't overly concerned as I felt I could work with anyone and be supportive of their challenges.

The first four months were unremarkable as we worked well together. In late February, she went out on a medical leave. Barbara provided the office with appropriate medical documentation for being off work. By the end of June, she had drawn down all of her leave balances and did not have any additional documentation to substantiate staying out of the office any longer.

In an effort to be proactive, I directed HR to draft a letter to be delivered certified mail stating the following: "To continue to remain off work on medical leave, employee must present a new doctor's note extending her time off. Employee needs to be aware of the fact that she has no further leave, therefore any additional time off will result in loss of pay. If employee plans on returning to work, she needs to immediately let me know. When employee's medical leave notice expires, she has five days to return to work or provide a new doctor's note or she will be separated from State service based upon her being absent without approval."

In the letter I also encouraged her to contact me so I could assist her based upon what her current circumstances were. My goal was to assist her in returning to work or ensure that she had the appropriate documentation to stay off work without jeopardizing her employment with the state and make her fully aware that, if she continued to remain off work, she understood she would not be receiving any pay.

I had no idea that while she was off work, she was not seeing her doctor, was not going to counseling, was not taking her medication, and had gotten on marijuana and methamphetamines. My two HR managers and I started receiving threatening phone messages from Barbara. She was extremely explicit in what her plans were for us. I directed HR to immediately contact the California Highway Patrol (CHP) who also serves in the role as police for state employees.

Upon listening to the recorded phone messages, CHP indicated that the calls would be considered terrorist threats and she would be arrested. Three CHP officers went to her residence and got into a scuffle with her which resulted in her receiving a black eye. She was arrested and booked into the county jail.

Living Through The Pain

After her arrest, the CHP officer in charge of our case met with us and explained in detail what he found at her home upon arresting her. She had binders and binders of materials which described what she wanted to do to us. She had copies of letters forwarded to the Governor and other state officials. She had drawn pictures of us and taped them to her walls. She had taken clothing and plugged all her house drains. She had marijuana and methamphetamines in her home, and her house was in great disarray. He felt she was psychologically in a dangerous place, and he was definitely concerned that she would attempt to hurt one of us.

With this new information I quickly worked on obtaining restraining orders for the three of us. While this wouldn't stop her if she really wanted to hurt us, if we saw her within 100 feet of the office building, we could call CHP and have her arrested. Within a few days she posted bond and was released.

At this point she knew she could no longer call us due to the restraining order, so she started sending threatening post cards to our office. She would write so hard as to actually cut the postcard, simulating the use of a knife. She had previously threatened in the phone messages to cut us up. In addition, with her using postcards, the Business Services staff who sorted the mail couldn't help but read what the postcards said. Now word was getting out to the staff.

The post cards were horrible. She talked about how she was going to cut us up and bury us in the Capitol rose garden. She wanted to cut our clitoris out. She said horrible things about how we looked and what our sexual preferences were, according to her. The post cards were wretched and left us shaking and scared. On any typical business day, the office could receive up to ten postcards.

One day we received a string of postcards referencing a blog site she had created. Naturally we went to the blog site where she referenced our home addresses and again her plans for us. Each blog referred to us as "bitches," "whores," "cunts," etc. Emotionally, we all were beginning to self-destruct under the continued pressure.

I fought with my boss to provide clear information to the staff to limit our possible liability should something occur. I also fought with him to get permission to hire security guards until this issue could be resolved. I went forward and posted a recent picture of Barbara and a description of her car and license plate number and scheduled a meeting with staff and the CHP officers to provide an open dialogue about what was happening, how to be prepared and what to do if someone saw her or her car. This didn't go over very well with my boss as he felt I was blowing it all out of proportion, stating I was a hormonal woman!

Truly, I didn't care, as I knew I had a responsibility to keep the staff informed and that I had needed to keep the office as secure as possible. The CHP officers met with the staff and clearly described the situation. They indicated that it was just a matter of time before she would do something. In their opinion, it wasn't an "If she would do something;" it was a "When was she going to do something." They also explained when they went out to arrest her the first time it took three officers to subdue her as with the methamphetamines and marijuana, she was uncontrollable. They warned staff to practice due diligence when it came to safety and being alert and prepared at all times. By now, she had been arrested several times, but was always bailed out. We had hoped they would hold her on a 5150, involuntary psychiatric hold, but the jail was already so overcrowded, they would release her on bail, so she wasn't getting the medical attention she needed.

Staff began to voice their concerns and how scared they were. I knew they were, and this added additional stress to me as I felt a responsibility to try and protect everyone. At this point I went around my boss and met directly with the Director of our department. I explained to him that in my opinion we could terminate her based upon the State policy of "zero tolerance" for workplace violence. He agreed. I further explained that we need to go to our Agency (Governor's Cabinet level) and ask their attorney to take over the case and notify her of the termination. I felt removing any decisions from our office would be best for the staff as a whole and would limit liability on the part of the department since then it wouldn't appear that we were retaliating against her. Again he agreed. He said he would contact Agency and speak to their attorney to provide us the necessary legal assistance we needed ASAP.

Every night after work I had one of my staff walked me to my car. I was scared to be alone in the parking lot as I usually left work around 6 to 6:30 and my staff person had a later schedule, so he also left around the same time. This particular night the staff person walked me to my car, then with tears in his eyes, he told me he couldn't walk me out anymore. I asked him why and he responded that he was scared he would be attacked as well because he was with me. I responded that I totally understood and gave him a big hug and thanked him for his honesty. Once I shut my car door I finally fell apart. I had been trying to hold it all in for weeks, but the fear had now risen to the level that I couldn't contain it anymore. I was worried about the staff and was naturally concerned for my two HR managers and myself.

All these years I had held my emotions in check. Now I felt I had slid slowly into the abyss. I had trouble driving home. Once home, I told my husband I couldn't do it anymore, that I needed help. I asked him to take me to the doctor the next day. I was no longer sleeping; I was constantly shaking, fearful of being by myself, throwing up, and emotionally I was a total wreck. The doctor immediately took me off work for two weeks.

After two weeks I returned to the office and it was time to attend the first hearing before the judge regarding her first arrest. I had Dusk come with me to the courthouse as I was scared to see her. She didn't show up. That was my last day in the office, as my doctor placed me on an extended leave through November and was having me see a clinical psychologist and psychiatrist to oversee the medication I needed to reduce my anxiety and panic attacks. I was diagnosed as having Post Traumatic Stress Disorder (PTSD). The doctor explained that, based upon my prior history with traumatic events coupled with this traumatic event, I emotionally couldn't handle the stress and pressure any longer.

I had no idea how far I would fall. As time went on I kept getting worse. I purchased a Taser gun for protection as I was scared all the time. I stayed in the house with the alarm turned on and had my son bring his dog over so there would be two dogs for protection. I remained curled up on the couch and in a zombie state based upon the medicines I was prescribed. The only times I ventured out of the house was for doctor's appointments as I wouldn't even go outside to pick up the mail. Every day I retreated further and further from this world into a place where I felt safe inside myself.

To make matters worse, the doctors messed up my medications. I initially started taking medicines prescribed by my primary care physician. Once I saw the psychiatrist, she took me off those medications and placed me on new medications.

I now know that a person must be weaned off anti-depressive medicine before his or her medicine can be changed. This didn't happen for me. Three weeks later I was getting worse, so the psychiatrist changed my medications yet again, only this time my insurance would not approve the new medicines. They placed a call into the psychiatrist for additional justification.

Only later would I find out that the psychiatrist didn't immediately call the insurance company back. An on duty psychiatrist called back and got the prescriptions approved. Later that day, my psychiatrist got the message and called in a different group of prescriptions for me in lieu of what the insurance would approve (or so she thought). When the pharmacy called to tell me my prescriptions were ready,

I picked up six prescriptions (all different) which resulted in my being over-medicated.

Little by little my thought process was eroding. When I went to a doctor's appointment I would get lost and have to call Dusk to have him remind me where I was supposed to be going. I banged up my car three times trying to parallel park it when I didn't have the faculties to do so. I fell asleep three different times while on the freeway. I was fortunate as I wasn't driving in rush hour traffic, so as I crossed over into the emergency lane, the change in pavement would jolt me awake. An angel had to seriously be watching over me during these months as I couldn't take care of myself.

Finally I was ready to return to work so I sent an email to my boss notifying him the date I would return. The very next day someone came to my house and rang the doorbell. I was terrified. I looked out and saw a courier service person and I asked what they wanted. The man replied he had a package to serve me which I had to sign for. I asked him to leave the package and the document I was to sign at the door and get back into his truck. I would then step out and sign for the package.

I was fortunate that he complied with my request. After signing and picking up the package, I went back inside, sat down on the couch, and prepared myself while opening the package. I assumed Barbara was suing me for her termination. I was so unprepared for what lay ahead that it sucked all the air out of my chest.

The package contained a letter signed by my boss (whom I had gone around). He was now the Acting Director of the department and he was firing me! My world exploded at that moment. I loved my job and felt I had worked hard for the department and had accomplished quite a bit in the short amount of time I had been there. I had put myself out there by agreeing to take on Barbara and had struggled to handle the situation as professionally as I could under extreme stress and anxiety, and now I had pushed myself hard to get ready to come back to work and I was fired.

Dusk was in training that day and my son was studying for his licensing test to become a certified engineer with the State. I knew I couldn't call either of them. I felt extremely suicidal and knew I needed immediate help. Looking back, I should have called 911, but I was incapable of thinking rationally.

I called my doctor, my psychiatrist, my clinical psychologist. I couldn't reach any of them. I then called three of my friends and no luck. I was getting desperate and starting to sweat profusely. I called Dusk's mom and finally got a hold of her. I cried to her about what had happened and that I couldn't control my thoughts. To me, this was the end of my world and I was going to commit suicide. Mom said should drive down for me to hold on and wait for her. She was two hours away. When she hung up she called her daughter, my sister-in-law Dawn, who immediately called me and calmly and softly spoke to me, calming me down until mom arrived at the door.

God was watching over me that day as if I wouldn't have gotten a hold of mom, I know I wouldn't be here today. I know I didn't want to die, but I couldn't handle anymore disappointments in my life and, with the over medication, I could not soundly and clearly think. It was too much for me to handle. No more; I didn't want to take anything else this world had to throw at me.

 I was so happy to have mom with me until Dusk got home. When I saw him, I lost it all again. I felt shameful having to tell him I had lost my job and placed us in a financial turmoil. He held me and told me not to worry, we would get through this. He got me to my clinical psychologist the following day. Losing my job was a big shock to my system and a huge setback in my recovery.

 About six weeks after being fired, one of the managers who used to work for me called me at home to let me know that Barbara had committed suicide. He had been told not to call me, yet he felt obligated to let me know so I wouldn't live the rest of my life always looking over my shoulder. I felt relief of not having to worry about Barbara hurting me or anyone else, but at the same time I grieved for her. She was a good person and someone I cared about.

 I was saddened that we tried to get her help when she was in jail, but the system failed her. There was no one there to provide her the assistance she needed. In my role with the State, I couldn't reach out compassionately to try and assist her. Besides, if I had tried, I could have triggered her into actually hurting me. I later found out she had been threatening her family members as well, so she had absolutely no support group left to help her. I wondered why it had to end this way.

 A few months later I woke up and started throwing up and realized that, when I tried to talk, I couldn't make sentences. My head was pounding, I was shaking, I was confused, and I could tell my heart was beating fast. I sent a cryptic email to Dusk indicating simply "come home" as I couldn't write anymore than that. He immediately called me, but I wasn't making any sense, so he rushed home.

By the time he got there, I was in bad shape. He called my clinical psychologist and explained my new symptoms. She did some follow up on the computer and called back, indicating it sounds like I am experiencing Serotonin Syndrome, a type of drug poisoning from being over-medicated. This reaction to being over-medicated can be fatal if not caught in time. She wanted him to immediately bring me in to see her and bring all my medicines. One she saw me she realized the doctors had messed up and had given me too many medicines for the same problems; in other words, I was being doubly medicated.

She referred me to a new psychiatrist. This new doctor evaluated and confirmed the diagnosis. He took me off all my medications and placed me on a medicine that is a form of Speed. Once again the drastic change shocked my system. I went four days without sleeping. It was a few weeks before I came out of the cloud and could think clearly, except now I was extremely hyper. I couldn't stop talking and doing things. This new doctor slowly brought me off Speed while replacing it some new medications. All of the changes triggered insomnia, which lasted for over two years. I would go several days without sleeping, and then would sleep for twenty hours straight. It was difficult to function.

Finally I was referred to a new psychiatrist. This doctor took great pains to work with me to get my emotional state calmed down and get me on a solid medication remedy without anymore abrupt changes. I saw this doctor for about one year before he quit accepting my insurance.

By this point I was for the most part stable, with few ups and downs. I was once again referred to a new psychiatrist who kept me on the same medicines. I finally returned to work to a different department working three hours a day and slowly building back to full-time.

As of the time of writing this book, I am working full-time, but typically miss one day a week for various issues such as migraines, inflammation, insomnia, joint stiffness, muscle spasms, vomiting, chronic fatigue, vertigo, etc. My body is still trying to work through all the various medicines that have been in my body, the enormous stress I was under, the complete emotional breakdown I had, and slowly getting used to trusting my environment and not experiencing panic attacks when voices are raised or there are loud noises. All of my doctors have confirmed that suffering from the PTSD is what triggered the horrible spiraling down path I experienced.

Somehow while off all those months, I found my courage to begin the process of writing this book. It seems odd that I had the courage to begin to reflect back over my life, but I didn't have enough strength to deal with the current realities of my life. Since I wasn't sleeping at night, I could spend numerous hours just typing away, pouring out my soul into the computer. I suppose this was the only way I knew how to begin the healing process.

As the months flashed by, I was slowly weaned off the numerous medicines. I was back to work in another state position and slowly working on rebuilding my health, my emotional state, and my life. I felt to have gone through all the ordeals I have had to face in my life; I could and should be able to handle anything that comes my way.

I am definitely much stronger and wiser for the traumas I have dealt with. I wouldn't want to go through any of them again, but I am grateful I now have a family support system and good doctors to assist me in the process, and my heart is right with God. I continually turn to him for guidance, strength and courage. Without my family support, good doctors, and my relationship with God, I know this last event would have put me in a psychological state that I wouldn't have recovered from. I feel blessed.

CHAPTER 24

My Never-Ending Love for My Father

"Love never ends. These three things continue forever: faith, hope, and love. And the greatest of these is love."

1 Corinthians 13:8, 13

A remarkable thing happened to me while in the process of writing this book which brought me keen awareness of my dad's accomplishments. In 1980 I graduated from Texas A&M University, proudly following in my father's and two older brothers' footsteps. As a result of being a former alumnus, I regularly receive a copy of the *Texas Aggie Magazine*. While reading the magazine in early May, 2013, I noticed an advertisement for the Distinguished Alumnus Award. For some reason I had never seen this award program.

Upon further review I discovered this award program was established in 1962 and is the highest honor bestowed upon a former student of Texas A&M University. The award recognizes former students who have made significant contributions to society and whose accomplishments and careers have brought honor and distinction to Texas A&M and The Association of Former Students.

It is funny how God works in our lives. God placed on me a heavy heart once I read about this award. I couldn't get the award out of my mind and how my father should be nominated. After a few days of battling with myself about this feeling, I finally called the award program contact who informed me that an individual could be honored posthumously; therefore I could nominate my father. This was exciting news, and at the same time it was overwhelming to me. I looked at the information which would need to be submitted and again my heart was heavy. I certainly knew my father was bigger than life, but what could I possibly bring together to explain my father's accomplishment, after all, I was sixteen when he died.

I could definitely write the nomination letter, but I needed to draft a biography on him and list awards received and provide a timeline of his achievements. Wow, I didn't have any of this. In addition, I had to have three support letters to accompany my packet. I felt defeated before I even started the project, yet God wouldn't release me from the constant tugging at my heart. Finally, I gave in and started doing research on the Internet trying to determine who could assist me with the three support letters. I started with this part of the project as I felt I wouldn't be able to go forward without the three letters.

I spent numerous hours conducting research, with

everything turning into a dead end. It seemed most people who knew my father had already passed away. I had no contacts at the radio or television stations. Every name I could think of, either I couldn't track them down or I discovered they were deceased. I was frustrated and felt defeated in my pursuit. I prayed nightly for God's direction and guidance. I felt if God wanted me to pursue this, He needed to provide me with some guidance.

One night it came to me that I should look in a box that contains a lot of family pictures. I don't have much, as my brother had gotten rid of most things related to my family. Going through this box, I came across some newspaper articles about the plane crash which provided me with some brief insight on my father's accomplishments, so this was a start; then I came across a letter from a lady who had known my father in connection with his work with the State of Israel.

She had written to congratulate my son for his college graduation, noting how proud my father would have been. The letter was ten years old, and I was worried that she, too, had passed on or might be in a nursing home by now. I sent an email to her based upon what was listed on her stationary and by the next day she responded by calling me. I was overjoyed.

Florence is her name, and she is quite a character. We spoke off and on for several weeks as she revealed different stories about my father. My pride in my father and his accomplishments continued to grow with each passing conversation. I couldn't help but cry every time we talked, then I would cry for several hours afterwards. How much I had missed about my father and what an awesome person he had been. Oh, how I wished my son could have known him. Florence went on to help me track down some contacts who could provide me with support letters. God indeed works miracles when a person prays.

More people started calling me and telling me stories about my father. I continued to learn more about him and felt so blessed at this point in the process that I realized even if my father's name wasn't selected, I had learned so much information after thirty-seven years since his death that it was a win-win either way.

Without God's constant nudge, I would have never ventured down this path, and I realized the blessing I would have lost. At a time in my life when connecting with my family became so important to me, God provided a channel to give me the connection I needed. I felt in touch with my family for the first time in years. For once when I dreamed, it was not about the plane crash, but rather positive interactions with them and with me being an adult. In my dreams I was able to connect with my father and hear from him that he was so proud of me. Even though it was only a dream, it was so special when I woke up as I keenly felt my father's presence.

I know it was no coincidence that this was the first time I ever noticed this awards program. Previously I wouldn't have been emotionally prepared to tackle this journey, yet now was the perfect time for me and was the right time to receive information on my father. In addition, my research took me to Texas A&M to contact them about my father's belongings.

I remembered that my brother told me he had boxed up everything in my father's office and donated it to A&M for a display at the University library. I never knew if he really did this or not, but now was my opportunity to find out. I was referred to several different people before I was put in contact with a lady over the University's archives. Upon her research she discovered several boxes of my father's material in storage. After some convincing, she assigned a student to provide me with a list of the items contained in boxes which provided substantive information for my father's biography.

In time I plan to write to the Director of the Library to make a formal request for my father's documents. I have already been told that once a donation is made, the documents then belong to the State of Texas since this is a State-sponsored University. I was also informed that it would be a rare exception if the University allowed me to take possession of my father's belongings, but I feel it is merely another challenge for me to embark upon.

I strongly believe there is a reason why, after all of these years, I have finally learned that there are belongings that the University has and what they are. I know God has led me to this discovery so I can connect with my father's history and provide that connection to my son.

By the time my book is published, I should know if my father is going to be one of the recipients of the award. I plan to continue to pray for this recognition of my father's accomplishments as it will be a legacy for my son and his children to take great pride in.

At the same time, this part of my journey has been so

rewarding for me. It has helped heal my heart in ways that previously hadn't been possible. I know my life has been hard and mostly has been a difficult uphill climb where at times I would slip and slide downhill.

Many times I felt overwhelmed and defeated and wanted to give up, yet God always gave me the strength to continue with my journey uphill even if it was at a slow pace. I believe that, once my book is published and released, I can finally take a break, breathe deeply and rest. I can take pride in my journey and get prepared with the hope that I can begin meeting with people who need inspiration as they have just embarked on their journey. I know this is my calling in life.

I know the path I have gone down is the path God planned for me. A Catholic priest once told me, after hearing my life story, that he had no words to help me with my journey, but he strongly felt my journey was that of God's design to help others. He felt I was provided with the strength and inner fortitude to remain positive in times of despair to keep me moving forward so in time I could help others. What a trip I have had. The journey has been no easy task, yet there have been many blessings throughout and, looking back, I can see God's handiwork in guiding, leading and carrying me along the path.

CHAPTER 25

Lessons Learned

"God uses adversity in the lives of his children. Adversity, however, is not simply a tool. It is God's most effective tool for the advancement of our spiritual lives. The circumstances and events that we see as setbacks are often times the very things that launch us into periods of intense spiritual growth."

Charles Stanley

I have learned a lot in my life thus far. First and foremost is to remember God loves you regardless of your sin. He hates the sin, but he loves the person. So when you mess up, which we all do, go to God and ask for forgiveness. He can heal your heart. If something doesn't feel right, don't go along with it. Even if it means you aren't cool or the guy won't like you or your friends think you are dumb, who cares? If it feels wrong, it is wrong. Never lie. The end never justifies the mean. There is nothing worth lying about. When they say, "The truth will set you free," it really does.

I have also learned to fully trust God, not to question

God's intentions, and to forgive those who have hurt me. This has provided peace in my life. I am no longer scared to die. I don't have to hold grudges, but rather forgive and pray for those who have hurt me. This brings light and peace to my life and keeps the darkness at bay. Life is good and God is good.

If I had confessed my sins about Christopher to God and then told my parents, I wouldn't have gone down the horrible path that I did. If I hadn't accepted a beverage with alcohol that I knew was wrong to drink, I would have never been alone with Christopher. If I had listened to my heart, I wouldn't have married Christopher. Being alone and by myself would have been a much better choice.

I did make those decisions, and I ended up in a bad marriage. I have made every effort to make things right when it came to raising my son. Was I perfect in all my decisions? Absolutely not, but the decisions and problems I took to God first always turned out right. Life has many unanswered questions; at least for me that is true. Why did my family die so young? Why did my surviving brother not want me? Why did he have to die? Why did no one reach out to me after the accident? I wasn't invited to spend the night or the weekend with anyone. I wasn't asked to go to the movies or to have dinner with someone, or even receive a call or a letter.

Why didn't my aunts help me? Why didn't my school ensure I got counseling? Why did my boyfriend and eventual husband treat me the way he did? Why was the divorce judge so harsh to me? Why didn't Christopher have any self-respect and act like a man when it came to the divorce, the bills, and child support? Why did Carl use me, and then cheat on me? If Steve was unhappy in his first marriage, why did he feel guilty after marrying me? Why, why, why?

I can conjure up answers, but the truth is this is just life. Tragedy happens; people fail one another, people don't know how to effectively communicate, people like free-rides and an easy way out. No one likes to take responsibility, and how can a person be expected to respect others when they have no self-respect for themselves? These are harsh, cold realities of life, but they are true. The sooner you realize this, the better off you will be. You can't sit and worry tirelessly over spilled milk; you just have to pick yourself up and move on.

God never promised life would easy, but He did promise salvation for us, which is far more important. As for me, I always figured God gave me a rough and rocky path to go down for a reason. I still don't know what that reason is, but I wouldn't change my life. I appreciate my father's love of agriculture, which I now have.

I feel close to God when I am surrounded by nature. I love to hear the birds sing, feel the sun on my face and the cool breeze gently blowing across my cheeks. The fragrance of the flowers in bloom and the leaves rustling in the trees reminds me that God is there. I have a deep sense of compassion for people, especially those who are abused or neglected. Due to the paths I have gone down, I also have the ability to feel and understand other people's pain.

CHAPTER 26

Moving Forward

"I tell you there is more joy in heaven over one sinner who changes his heart and life, than over ninety-nine good people who don't need to change."

Luke 15:7

Everybody needs a shoulder to lean on, someone to trust and to know that someone has your back. I am that someone. I try to help people with their pain, with their feelings of inadequacy or their inability to love. Love is the most powerful emotion God gave us. To feel love and compassion toward others brings it right back to you. The same is true about hate. It is so toxic. To fill your life with hate only contaminates your soul with anger and darkness. There is no room for light, love, and peace when you are bitter and resentful. Let it go and good things will come your way.

"A life without problems or limitations or challenges—life without 'opposition in all things,' as Lehi phrased it

(2 Nephi 2:11) *would paradoxically but in fact be less rewarding and less ennobling than one which confronts even frequently confronts difficulty and disappointment and sorrow,"* Created for Greater Things, Jeffrey R. Holland.

"*This one thing I do, forgetting those things which are behind, and reaching forth unto those things which are before, I press toward the mark . . ."* (Philippians 3:13–14). This is the secret to finding peace in your life. We all make mistakes. Even David, one of the greatest Kings in the Bible, committed adultery and murder, yet God showed him favor as he repented for his sins and asked for forgiveness. If we learn from our mistakes and honestly take our sins to God and ask for forgiveness with a pure heart, God will forgive and the sin is no more. It is hard for someone like me to let go of the sin, release the shame, and stop the constant punishing of myself for falling short, but once I took hold of the above scripture and released it to God, my sins were forgiven. I just needed to forgive myself. That goes back to the self-reconciliation concept. One of the most blessed gifts you can give yourself is to forgive yourself. Accept your past, learn from your mistakes, and move on with your life.

"*The past is to be learned from but not lived in. We look back to claim embers from glowing experiences but not the ashes. And when we have learned what we need to learn and have brought with us the best that we have experienced, then we look ahead; we remember that faith is always pointed toward the future,"* Created for Greater Things, Jeffrey R. Holland

Also remember that dying is part of the life cycle. We

all have one thing in common—we all are going to die. When I asked Dusk why God took my family, he told me, "God sometimes takes the most beautiful flowers in the garden." Oh, for my family that made so much sense. Heaven is so much more special having my precious family there and, besides, they are waiting for me. Until then I have several guardian angels looking over me.

I thank God for my blessings each and every day. My parents provided a solid core foundation built upon God. My family taught me love of nature and hard work. My mother taught me how to provide love unconditionally to my son and to make him my priority. Ronnie taught me how to enjoy life with laughter. My beautiful sister-in-law taught me about the beauty that God has provided within each of us, and finally Kerry taught me how to forgive. I have been blessed with an awesome family to have come from, a son who means the world to me, and a husband who loves me for me, even with my faults.

We never know what tomorrow will bring. One day you might find yourself as a lonely figure kneeling in the dark with tears streaming down your face. What I do know is you are not alone. God is right there. Turn to him even if you are scared. You may not have a family member or a friend or a co-worker to turn to or to trust, but you can always count on God. I can now see He was always walking beside me, carrying me sometimes and holding me at other times, but He was always there, even when I didn't turn to him. With God, you can "live through the pain."

Photos

The Compton Family: Ronnie, Kerry, Dewey, Curtis and Cathy

Dewey Compton

Living Through The Pain

Curtis Compton

Cathy A. Kurtz

Ronnie Compton

Living Through The Pain

Kerry Compton

The Compton kids with sister-in-law *June 1976*

Hearses at funeral

Compton Family caskets

Cathy Compton's High School graduation picture

Nick at 5 years old

Cathy and Dusk's wedding *June 13, 1998*

www.ingramcontent.com/pod-product-compliance
Lightning Source LLC
Chambersburg PA
CBHW030321080526
44584CB00012B/658